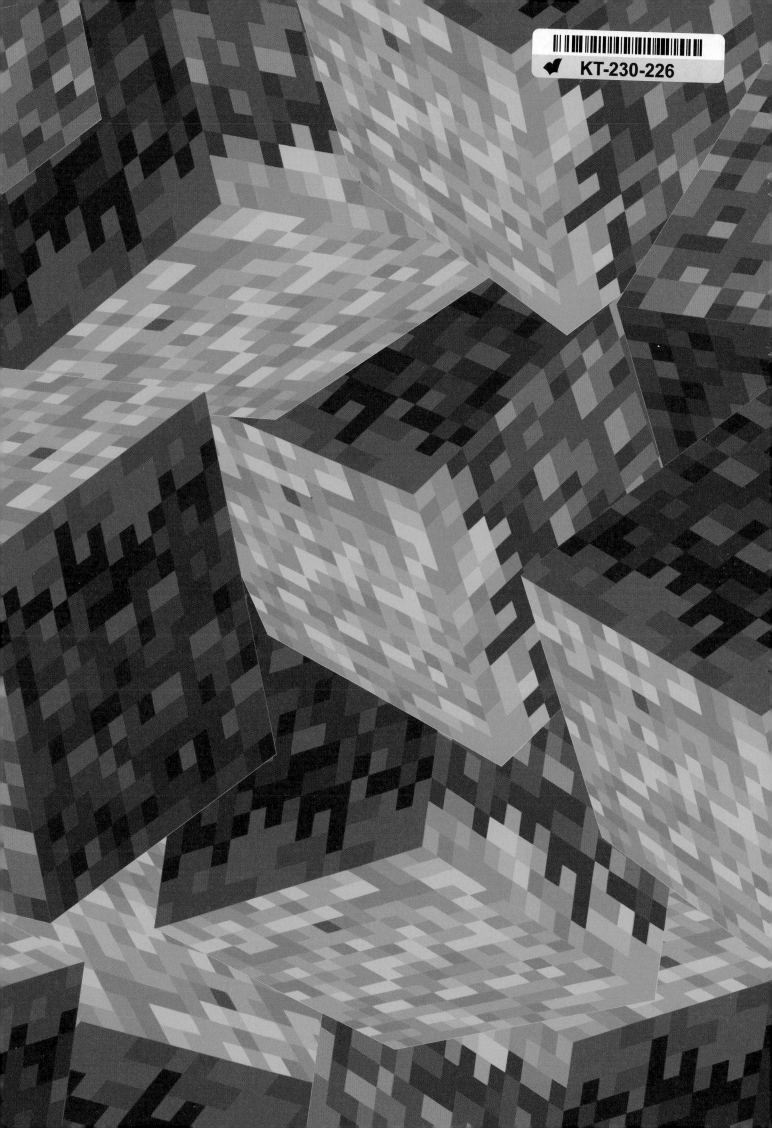

GAMES MASTER

PRESENTS

MINECRAFT

PUZZLES

Customising Minecraft

PAGE 48

Make your game just the way you like it and supercharge your Minecraft experience!

PAGE 38

HOW TO DEFEAT CREEPERS

LittleBrother

Published 2018

Little Brother Books Ltd
Ground Floor, 23 Southernhay East, Exeter, Devon, EX1 1QL

Printed in Poland

books@littlebrotherbooks.co.uk
www.littlebrotherbooks.co.uk

HOW TO PLAY
MINECRAFT
IN 3D
PAGE **64**

SETTING UP YOUR GAME AND GETTING THE MOST FROM 3D!

PAGE
12
BUILD AN
AT-AT
WALKER

inside...

DIFFICULTY

★ ★ ★

NORMAL
WITH A BIT OF TIME AND PATIENCE, EVERYONE CAN DO THIS

2 1/2 HOURS

IT LOOKED LIKE THIS BEFORE!

AND THEN LIKE THIS AFTER OUR MAGIC!

JUST SEE HOW MUCH A VILLAGE CAN IMPROVE IN THESE BEFORE AND AFTER PICS!

Load your Hotbar with...
- Cobblestone
- Stone Bricks
- Stone Brick Stairs
- Stone Half Slabs
- Lava Bucket
- White Terracotta
- Dark Oak Wood
- Dark Oak Planks
- Dark Oak Wood Stairs
- Cracked Stone Bricks
- Glass Panes
- Cobweb
- Water
- Cobblestone Wall
- Leaves
- Hoe
- Wheat
- Stone Buttons
- Armour Stand
- Torches

SUPERCHARGE A VILLAGE!

Villages might naturally spawn, but they're not naturally attractive. We show you how to remodel them into something fantastic!

ARE YOU LOCAL?

WHEN YOU create a new world in Minecraft, villages will naturally spawn in a random way in desert, taiga, savanna and plains biomes. Each biome will create a village in its own style, but none of them are that attractive. We're going to show you ways to demolish and rebuild key parts of your chosen Village – improve the Blacksmith's Forge, sort out those pesky Iron Golem – supercharge your village!

INFO

SUPERCHARGE A VILLAGE

TIME NEEDED: 2 1/2 HOURS
EXTRA INFO: YOU CAN CHOOSE YOUR OWN STONE AND WOOD BLOCKS IF YOU LIKE

1

SEARCH FOR A VILLAGE

FIND YOURSELF a lovely village that's ripe for a makeover. Chances are when you find one the ground there is going to be a mess thanks to the way Minecraft spawns villages. Let's kick things off by mining up all the Grass and Dirt in-between all the buildings so we have a nice flat surface to work with.

2
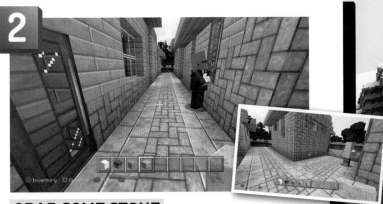

GRAB SOME STONE

WITH THE ground all even, arm yourself with some Cobblestone and Stone Bricks. We're using the City texture pack on the PlayStation 4, but feel free to use whichever pack you like. Next run the Stone Bricks around the outside edge of the pathway area, then in the gap in the middle lay down some Cobblestone.

3

FIND THE BLACKSMITH

HEAD TO where the Blacksmith's Forge has spawned inside your chosen village. Every village in Minecraft is unique, so where it will be will likely be different to ours. Once you've found it, smash up the Forge, mine up the roof, and clear the whole space out so all you're left with is the ground beneath.

4

CHARGE THAT HOTBAR

ADD SOME Stone Stairs to your hotbar and create a 4x4 square with them. Knock out each of the corners then head to the front side and mine that up, too. With Stone Stairs in hand, run a row of outward-facing Stairs next to one another. This area is where the Lava will go, but not quite yet!

5

STONE BRICKS

YOU SHOULD now be left with 3 solid Stone Brick rows and 1 row of Stairs. Look towards the Stone Brick rows. Ignoring the middle block on each side for the moment, place down Stone Stairs facing outward on each of the ends. Now go ahead and fill in the middle of the Stairs with Stone Bricks. Starting to look good!

6

REBUILDING WORK

ON EACH of the middle blocks you just placed down, add another set of Stairs facing away on top of the structure. Next to each step, on the side, lay down some Stone Bricks. When you view what you're building from above it should look like you're filling in the inside corners. The new Forge is starting to take shape!

7

KEEP BUILDING UP

YOUR BRAND-spanking new Blacksmith's Forge will be looking a little bit weird at the moment. Don't worry, it's not finished yet! Looking to the 4 Stone Bricks from the last step, drop Stairs on top of them and connect them so you're left with a cross shape on top. If in doubt, check out the picture above that shows you where to put the blocks.

8

A SMASHING TIME

NEXT WE'RE going to mine up those 4 corner Stairs. Head inside the Blacksmith's Forge, and when you've worked out which blocks are the 4 inside corners, smash them to bits – that's a real fun bit! You should end up with a small gap from where they were, so let's cover that with Stone Half Slabs.

9

WATCH OUT – LAVA!

GRAB A Lava Bucket and fill in the bottom. Then with Stone Bricks, create a chimney poking out of the cross section you just built. And with that your master Blacksmith's Forge is complete and looking mighty fine. We'll be sprucing the rest of it up later, but for now, give yourself a pat on the back.

10

HOME IMPROVEMENTS

NOW IT'S time for some home makeovers for those village houses. Find the 'L' shape house if possible (although any house will do). Knock out the walls and replace them with White Terracotta. Then with Dark Oak Wood, mine each of the corners of the house and build spikes in their place.

11

ROOF REBUILDING

COMPLETELY DEMOLISH the roof and then build up the walls by 5 blocks, again with White Terracotta. Head back to the Dark Oak Wood and continue the spikes up the sides of the new walls. When that's all done, connect the Dark Oak horizontally to create a frame effect. You can see what we mean in the smaller pic above.

12

A NEW COLOUR

FOR THIS next step we'll be putting the roof back on in a different shade to make it look more impressive. Grab Dark Oak Planks and run them along the front-top of the house and along the back-left side. Next create a step effect going up. The front section should be 8 blocks high, while the back is just 6 blocks tall.

13

STAIRS INTO A ROOF

WITH SOME Dark Oak Wood Stairs, extend the front section so it becomes parallel with the beginning of the back section. Then, extend the back section across the house. After that's all connected, finish by running Stairs 1 block below the entire roof and add in windows in the centre of each section.

14

SIMILAR, BUT DIFFERENT

OF COURSE, every village has multiple houses, so let's pick another one at random, and repeat what we did in the last few steps. This time start with the roof – mine up 1 block, replace with Dark Oak, and repeat until it's completed. Finish by digging up the walls and replacing them with Terracotta.

15

MIX IT UP

YOU CAN always leave this until later, but now is a great time to makeover all the remaining houses so they match the previous ones we just showed you how to do. If you fancy a different design to break up all the white, try changing the walls to a mix of Stone Bricks and Cracked Stone Bricks.

THE IRON GOLEM

YOU DON'T want to make an enemy out of an Iron Golem. These giant statues can spawn in villages if there is a 16x16x16 clear area, centred on the 21 or more houses in the village and if there are at least 10 villagers living there. 1 Iron Golem has a chance of spawning every 6 minutes.

BEING 2.7 blocks tall and 1.4 blocks wide, these giants can deliver a devastating blow if you annoy them. They LOVE the villagers, and if you attack a villager, or the Golem, they will come after you! One hit will cause between 7 and 21 damage to your heart meter and send you flying into the air!

THE BEST way of dealing with an Iron Golem is to simply run away! Keep out of their reach for a short time and they will forget about you and calm down. If you want to kill them off though, the most effective methods are lava, fire, cacti, poison or suffocation – they are hard nuts to crack! You can attack them with regular weapons, but you need to be close.

TRY MAKING a pit – an enclosed area where you can start a fire across the floor. If you can lure an Iron Golem into it, it will only last a minute before popping! Lava is even more effective, they can only last 13 seconds in lava. They don't like the spikes on Cacti either. More complicated is suffocation. It can be achieved by making a trap that has pistons placed to squash the Iron Golem, squeezed of breath they will only last around 25 seconds.

16

WRECKING BALL!

IT'S NOW time to go back to our Blacksmith's Forge that we rebuilt earlier on. See that cabin on the right? Wreck it. In its place, build walls on the right and back sides, add in Dark Oak like we did for our houses, and add a layer of Stone Half Slabs on top. It's all about upgrading the materials used in each building.

17

ADD SOME WINDOWS

EXTEND THE roof and Dark Oak frame so it goes all the way around the Blacksmith's Forge area. After you've laid down the Half Slabs on top, dig out a cross-shaped hole directly above the Forge. Lastly, add in windows around the structure – we used Glass Panes, but Glass blocks also work.

18

A SMOKING CHIMNEY

HEAD TO the cross-shaped hole and with Stone Bricks, extend the chimney of the Forge up into the air by 4 blocks. Run Half Slabs around the base of where the chimney pokes out, then with Cobwebs create a step effect coming from the top of the chimney so it looks like smoke coming out!

19

SMARTEN UP THE INSIDE

HEAD TO the inside, and in the right section, mine the floor and lay down a Cobblestone and Stone Brick pattern to match our village paths. Then add a single Stone step to act as a chair, and create a cooling pit by laying down a rectangle of Half Slabs and fill the inside with Water.

20

WELL, WELL, WELL!

FIND THE village Well – they all have one hidden somewhere – because we're going to spruce it up so it's less boring as 'well'! When found, destroy it (and get rid of the Water!). Next create a Stone Brick 'L' shape, leaving the front section open by 1 block. The diameter should be 3x3 blocks when viewed from above.

21

TAKE YOUR TIME

GET OUT your Stone Brick Stairs once more and run them around the outside of the 'L' shape. This next bit is tricky, so take it slowly to get it right. Lay Stairs on top of the other Stairs, only upside down this time. What you should be left with is a kind of 'C' shape going around the 'L' shape.

22

LOOKING GOOD

WITH SOME Cobblestone Wall, build on top of the 'L' shape by 2 blocks making 4 sets of pillars, then create a solid 2 block high cube. On the upper part of the cube, run Stairs around the outside and mine up the corners. Place 4 Stairs facing outwards on the cube, with a Half Slab in the middle, and that's it!

23

LEAVES & BLOCKS & LEAVES & BLOCKS

JUST LIKE the Well, the naturally spawning village farming areas aren't the best. So let's fix that right now. With Leaves and Dark Oak Wood, create the shape in the picture above. It's essentially 1 Dark Oak Wood block followed by 2 Leaves blocks (the entire shape would be 12x7 if fully completed, if that's easier for you to follow).

24

THE VEGETABLE PATCH

EXTEND EACH of the Dark Oak blocks up by 1. On top of the Leaves, grab Dark Oak Fence and run it between the wood. Then with a Hoe plant some vegetation of your choosing (we went with Wheat). Adding some more decorative bits, use Stone Buttons added to each of the Dark Oak blocks.

25

CREEPER WATCH

TO ROUND out our supercharged village project, all we need is a decent lookout post to watch for those Creepers! Create a 4x4 Stone Brick square somewhere overlooking the Village. Mine the corners, and replace with Dark Oak. Next, build the walls up really high, so you can see the entire village from the top.

26

KEEP A LOOKOUT

AT THE very top of your new tower run Dark Oak Half Slabs around the outside. On top of the Half Slabs, add in a ring of Dark Oak Fence too – you don't want to fall off! Next, build the inside corners – the Dark Oak corners – up by 5 blocks. An Armour Stand with a Steve's head could go here, too!

27

THE FINISHING TOUCH

GRAB YOUR Stairs for the final time and run them on top of the Dark Oak to create a square. 1 block in and up 1 block, add another smaller square made of Stairs. Keep doing this until you reach the top. Add Torches to the Fence and your village makeover is both complete *and* looking super-awesome – well done!

60 MINUTES!

AT-AT WALKER

Rebuild the classic Star Wars combat walker in Minecraft!

IF YOU ASK ME, THEY LOOK LIKE GIANT COWS!

DIFFICULTY

NORMAL
TAKE THE BUILD STEP-BY-STEP
AND YOU'LL FEEL THE FORCE!

START HERE!

1 FOR THIS build we'll be building multiple sections as we go. Start with 4, 5x5 cubes for the feet. Add 2x3 sections on each of the 4 sides, then drop a single Stone Half Slab in the centre of them. On top of the cube, lay a 3x3 flat section, and build the hook shape on top.

2 FROM THE centre of the hook shape, drop a row of 3 Black Wool. With Stone build in front of and to the sides of the Wool, then drop a 3 wide platform directly above. In the middle of that platform, build a 5 high spike out of Black Wool and build the corners up around it.

3 FOR THE gearbox, build a circle that's 5 blocks wide, a diagonal single block, then 5 blocks up. Continue the formation until it joins back on itself. Make the circle so it's 3 deep, then in the middle lay Black Wool from corner-to-corner. Put Stone around the Black Wool and that's it done.

4 FOR THIS next part we're going to build another of the spiked columns from step 2, and another of the gearboxes from step 3, directly above the last ones we built. At this point, it's worth remembering we're working on all 4 legs of the AT-AT Walker all at once.

5 WITH ALL 4 legs created, join the tops of the upper gearboxes together. Find the centre and create a step effect going down 3 levels. Add Black Wool 1 block behind the gaps to create some depth. Build it down 3 blocks. Then fill in the walls around it. Then do it again on the opposite side of the AT-AT Walker.

6 FROM THE middle step area, build up by 13 blocks to make a guideline. Next, build up the other sides of the guideline so you have a solid wall on each side of the Walker. Next build another 2 high wall 1 block in on the top, and add in the shapes with Black Wool behind them.

7 FILL IN the back and front of the Walker with Stone, and for the neck, run a single block panel behind a second panel that's 1 block bigger. For the head, build a square 22x14 massive wall and knock off blocks to create the shapes in the picture.

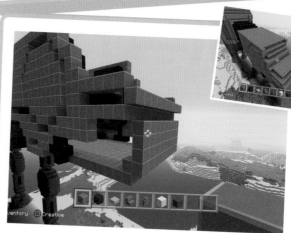

8 NOW FOR the front of the face. Head to behind the Black Wool cross and build 9 blocks along. Create a smaller panel 1 block above and out at the end that's 4 blocks high. Move inside the head and fill the floor, then start connecting all the walls round to one another.

BUILD THIS!

9 FOR THE final part: giant cannons! From the black crosses, build cannons out of Grey Wool, Black Wool, Dispensers, and Buttons. Build a row of Black Wool underneath the chin, then build 2 more cannons. And lastly, add more cannons to the massive circle areas on each side of the Walker's head.

ERR... LUCKILY NO-ONE DID ASK YOU, PAT! MAY THE FORCE BE WITH YOU...

PUZZLES

Test your brains with these teasers...

CIRCLE ALL THE DIFFERENCES ON PHOTO 2!

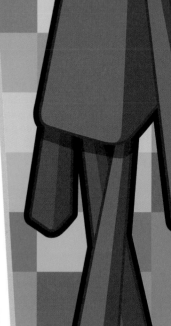

1

2

SPOT THE DIFFERENCE

TAKE A look at these two photos of Alex, Steve and their pet pig Percy! Can you spot the 6 differences between the two photos? Here's a clue... pigs only have two eyes!

WHAT'S FOR TEA?

SEE IF you can find the following 19 items in this wordsearch grid, shaped like one secret Food item! The remaining letters at the end should reveal the name of this item, which you're having for your tea (they're best used in Potions really though, and taste horrible!)

- ☑ EMERALD
- ☐ SLIMEBALL
- ☐ STRING
- ☐ CLOWNFISH
- ☑ CAKE
- ☑ BREAD
- ☐ SUGAR
- ☐ STICK
- ☐ COOKIE
- ☐ WHEAT
- ☐ PAPER
- ☐ MILK
- ☐ CAULDRON
- ☐ EGG
- ☐ BLAZEROD
- ☐ BOOK
- ☐ FEATHER
- ☐ QUILL
- ☐ FLINT

TICK OFF THE WORDS AS YOU FIND THEM!

ANSWERS ON PAGE 93

THE MYSTERY FOOD IS...

Puzzles

WORDBLOCKS

THESE NINE blocks each hide a secret 9-letter word connected to Minecraft. If you can un-jumble what the words are, reading in every direction, you'll find that the first letters of all 9 words spell out a bonus word! What is it?

WOOF! WHAT COULD THE BONUS WORD BE?!

ANSWERS ON PAGE 93

THE BONUS WORD IS...

☐ ☐ ☐ ☐ ☐ ☐ ☐ ☐ ☐

1

S	R	V
G	E	I
A	L	L

☐☐☐☐☐☐☐☐☐

2

B	L	E
I	S	I
I	N	V

☐☐☐☐☐☐☐☐☐

3

E	D	N
L	A	N
D	I	O

☐☐☐☐☐☐☐☐☐

4

E	E	R
N	D	M
E	T	I

☐☐☐☐☐☐☐☐☐

5

T	B	O
A	I	G
N	I	N

☐☐☐☐☐☐☐☐☐

6

R	P	N
E	O	U
D	W	G

☐☐☐☐☐☐☐☐☐

7

A	R	E
D	U	T
V	E	N

☐☐☐☐☐☐☐☐☐

8

O	N	E
T	S	O
S	S	M

☐☐☐☐☐☐☐☐☐

9

A	N	E
H	N	T
C	D	E

☐☐☐☐☐☐☐☐☐

10 MINUTES!

Build

OOO...
I'D LOVE TO HAVE A SWIM IN THIS POOL!

SWIMMING POOL

Splish, splash in this wet and wild build!

DIFFICULTY

EASY
THIS BUILD STARTS OUT EASY, BUT YOU CAN ADD TO IT!

START HERE!

1 SWIMMING POOLS are easy – they're just holes in the ground filled with water, right? True, but making them look like they do in real life takes a bit more creative Minecraft skill. In our example here, we have given the walls of our pool a chequerboard effect using Sea Lanterns, Blue Stained Glass and Glowstone behind to shine through for effect.

2 YOU CAN make your swimming pool as big or as small as you like to compliment your Minecraft world, ours is 12x7 blocks. We finished off the outside of our pool with Stone Slabs and Quartz Blocks so that is has that holiday-hotel-pool feel to it. You could even add some sunbeds!

3 NOW TO fill the swimming pool with Water. To make the Water flow properly, we need to put in a layer of blocks just beneath the Stone Slabs, then place Water Buckets on top of these blocks. Finally break the blocks and the water will fill the swimming pool.

4 FINISHING TOUCHES can turn a simple Minecraft build into a super Minecraft build. Here we have finished off our pool with 3 sizes of diving board – good enough for Tom Daley! The water looks so inviting shimmering away on a hot summer's day – dive right in!

BUILD THIS!

17

A MINECRAFT STORY

LORD OF ALL THE THINGS is the title of this exciting Minecraft story – and if you feel this tale has any similarities to another classic story... well, you may be right, but this is better, because it's MINECRAFT!

I've lost count of how many times I've got lost. I know the general direction of where I live – it's somewhere in that direction – maybe, probably, hopefully! But I might be just a tiny bit lost. Being lost isn't always the end of the world. Sometimes, when you're really lost, you end up finding something new, something exciting. In this case, I found a crumbling temple, and deep within, an artefact known as The One Thing, along with an inscription: "Whomever holds The One Thing will be Lord of All the Things."

Scary stuff! I'd been travelling for longer than I care to remember; venturing over frozen wastes, hot wastes, and cow waste. Days turned to weeks turned to months, and at last I'd found something to turn things around. But it appeared I wasn't the only one seeking their fortune. When I left the temple, a shadowy figure of legend, a Thingwraith, rode up on a skeletal steed. "Leave the Thing, pretender. It is not yours to take." I stood there, rooted to the ground as fear coursed through me, until I replied, "Nah, mate, it's mine now." The Thingwraith squealed like a pig under water and charged at me. I needed to run very fast!

I leapt from the temple and came crashing down on a snowy mound below. But my quick thinking didn't buy me much time. As I got to my feet, the Thingwraith came galloping over the side of the mountain and landed in front of me, its iron sword gleaming in the sunlight. The creature climbed down from its mount and skulked over to me. It raised its sword high above its head, before swinging it fiercely down. I held The Thing up to try and block it, and as sword met Thing, the wraith was sent back with a shockwave blast. I looked down at my body, only to find, somehow, some way, I was now invisible!

I ran and ran, then ran some more. Eventually I lost sight of the Thingwraith, though I knew it wouldn't give up chase completely. Hours later I found myself in a thriving

A story of temples, weird creatures and special powers!

city. Unsure what to do about my predicament, I sought out a wizard named Gandolph Ziggler. He was a bit of a show-off, but he told me The One Thing wasn't just an artefact, it was cursed. Typical, eh? You find something cool and then a grown-up says you can't keep it.

Between being chased by an undead monster in a black dress and finding out my new toy is cursed, I decided I should probably ditch it. Oh well. Being invisible wasn't that cool anyway... I asked Gandolph how I should go about destroying it, to which he said, "Throw it in the coldest, hottest place in all of Centre-Earth." How can something be cold and hot? That didn't make any sense! Or at least it didn't until I peered behind the city walls where amidst a snow-covered mountain lay a volcano.

Days passed, and with every passing hour I could feel the Thingwraith's icy breath growing ever closer. My feet hurt, my shoes were little more than scraps, and for once, I really fancied a hot bath. Nevertheless, I continued until I reached the volcano. I fought the ferocious heat to venture to its top, and as I held The One Thing over the lava, the Thingwraith appeared on the other side. "NO! That is mine, give it back!" I was too tired to fight, so instead, I blew it a kiss and lobbed The One Thing into the volcano. "NOOOO!" the Thingwraith wailed as it dived head-first into the lava after The Thing. There's a lesson here about not taking things that don't belong to you. But to be honest, all I can think about is that lovely hot bath with my name on.

Beware of wizards - they are always show-offs!

Cool, but hot? It could only be a volcano! Or Chilli Con Carne!

Make it!
MINECRAFT JOKE MACHINE

Cut out and fold the Minecraft Joke Machine then test it out on your friends! You'll soon be howling with laughter!

1 CUT OUT AND KEEP

FIRST THINGS first. Ask a grown up if you are okay to use the scissors, they don't need to be mega-sharp – just good enough to cut our book pages! Cut out the big square on the next page by following the dashed line around the outside. You can see it's made up of a series of squares with coloured panels, Mobs and jokes. Once you're done folding it you will have yourself a working Minecraft Joke Machine to try out on your friends!

WARNING!

ASK MUM, DAD, OR WHOEVER LOOKS AFTER YOU TO HELP WITH SHARP SCISSORS!

2 FLIPPING OVER

TURN THE square over and fold the four corners in to the centre of the square, along the solid blue lines. Now flip your smaller square back over again to the side with the jokes on it and fold in the four corners once more, on the dashed red lines. Next, fold your even smaller square in half, so that the coloured block panels are on the outside. Give it a good crease, then unfold it and do this again the other way, again remembering to give it a good crease.

3 OPENING UP

YOU NOW need to carefully slip your thumbs and forefingers under the coloured panels to open them up to create your Minecraft Joke Machine. Tease the contraption open by pushing and pinching with your thumbs and fingers. You want to loosen it up to get it ready for action! Now you're ready to test it out!

HOW TO PLAY

WITH YOUR Minecraft Joke Machine nice and loose, slip your fingers and thumbs inside and ask a friend to choose one of the coloured panels. You must spell out the colour of the panel, pulling and pinching your Joke Machine each time as you say the letters of the colour. For example, Yellow will be 6 moves.

IT'S THE WAY YOU TELL 'EM!

NEXT ASK your friend to choose a Minecraft Mob and again do the pulling and pinching movement to spell out the Mob's name. Alex, for example, would be 4 moves while Mooshroom would be a whopping 9! Finally, ask them to choose a second Mob from the open Joke Machine and open up the flap to reveal the joke underneath – tell the joke to your friend. Can they guess the punchline? If not, tell them with a straight face... no giggling!

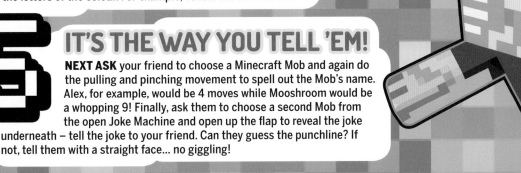

DID YOU HEAR THE ONE ABOUT THE...

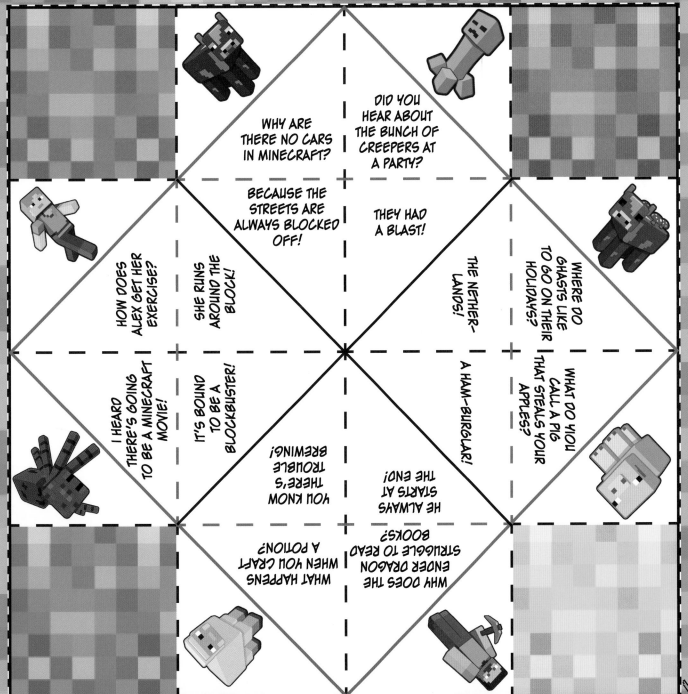

WHY ARE THERE NO CARS IN MINECRAFT?

DID YOU HEAR ABOUT THE BUNCH OF CREEPERS AT A PARTY?

BECAUSE THE STREETS ARE ALWAYS BLOCKED OFF!

THEY HAD A BLAST!

HOW DOES ALEX GET HER EXERCISE?

SHE RUNS AROUND THE BLOCK!

THE NETHER-LANDS!

WHERE DO GHASTS LIKE TO GO ON THEIR HOLIDAYS?

I HEARD THERE'S GOING TO BE A MINECRAFT MOVIE!

IT'S BOUND TO BE A BLOCKBUSTER!

A HAM-BURGLAR!

WHAT DO YOU CALL A PIG THAT STEALS YOUR APPLES?

YOU KNOW THERE'S TROUBLE BREWING!

HE ALWAYS STARTS AT THE END!

WHAT HAPPENS WHEN YOU CRAFT A POTION?

WHY DOES THE ENDER DRAGON STRUGGLE TO READ BOOKS?

21

ENJOY THE STORY

THIS GAME is a story, with the outcome and storylines affected by the choices you make along the way. So enjoy the journey and be sure to listen carefully to what the characters have to say. You can even play the game over and make new choices the second or third time!

EXPLORE AROUND

EACH LOCATION can have hidden booty. Be sure to open all the chests to find items that will be useful in your adventure, things you can click and examine will highlight as you pass the crosshairs over them and some have multiple options of what you can do with them. There's a lot of information and cool jokes to be discovered as you play, so click away at all highlighted items!

GOTTA BE QUICK

ACTION SEQUENCES in the game are controlled by what is called 'Quick Time Events'. This means you have to press the buttons that flash up on screen as quickly as possible as the action is happening. Make sure you know where all the buttons are before things get too scary out there!

MINECRAFT STORY MODE TOP TIPS!

Here are tips to get you started in Episode One of Story Mode...

CHICKEN CHAOS

YOU WILL come to a point in the story where you need to create some chicken chaos to distract the usher away from the door into the main hall. Luckily there's a man with a chicken machine on show at Endercon, but you can't get close enough to the window to smash it. Find the stall giving away Slime blocks to get 8 of them, but you need 9. Hopefully you made friends with Lukas before as he has the ninth one that will allow you to craft a Slime block and bounce your way up to the chicken window! Cluck, cluck!

WOAH, A WITHER!

WHAT STARTS out as a regular Wither soon gets out of control when Ivor's potion makes it stronger and turns it into a Wither Storm! You're going to be pressing buttons to avoid the swipes of the Wither as you all escape to Gabriel's fortress, but then you're given full control over where to run. The trick here is to avoid the tractor beams coming down from the Wither – dodge left and right when they come close to you. There are obstacles all over the ground too, so keep a close eye on the distance to see what's coming up next – and avoid it!

SAVING LUKAS

YOU DON'T have what it takes to rescue Lukas from the Iron Golem by brute force – he's big! Instead you need to think clever. Find a Potion Bottle to pick up and throw it at the Shelf with other bottles on it. This will cause the Iron Golem to stagger towards the shelf giving enough time for Lukas, Ruben and you to escape!

ACCURACY IS NEEDED

NOW YOUR clicking or tapping accuracy is going to be put to the test. The giant Wither Storm creature has tentacles that are out to get your friends. You can only stop it by swiping with your sword at them when prompted. The thing is you literally only have a few seconds to make your swipe before it's too late, so get ready with that finger, mouse or joypad as speed is everything here.

NETHER MIND

NOW FOR our favourite part of this first episode of Story Mode – the minecart ride! We think every game should have a minecart ride. It's a case of ducking when told to avoid hitting your head, but then a tricky lever must be hit to avoid the minecarts running into the lava. It is coming up on the right side of the minecart, so be ready with your crosshairs. You don't want to know what happens if you miss this lever!

I FEEL PIG SICK!

DIFFICULTY

NORMAL
MAP 1 IS EASY, BUT THE
FIREFIGHTING IN MAP 2 IS TRICKY

INSTRUCTIONS TO
INSTALL THE MAPS ARE
ON THE MUSEUM
WEBSITE!

THE GREAT FIRE OF LONDON!

3 hot maps from the Museum of London to download and spray with water!

THE GREAT FIRE 1666

TIME NEEDED: 10+ HOURS
EXTRA INFO: THREE
DOWNLOADABLE MAPS FROM
THE MUSEUM OF LONDON

FIRE! FIRE! It's 1666 and the city of London is on fire. It all started in a bakery in Pudding Lane when some smouldering embers caught alight and set the wooden building on fire, quickly spreading to next door. Around the bakery there were barrels of tar and brandy which helped the flames take hold!

Who said history was boring, eh? The boffins at the Museum of London have got together with a team of Minecraft experts to create not one, not two, but three hot (oh yes, they're hot!) maps of London 352 years ago

– and we've got top tips on playing all three. There's something here for all skill levels.

🔥 **Map 1** is called Pre Fire and teaches you what happened back in 1666.
🔥 **Map 2** is called The Fire and has you running around putting out the fire.
🔥 **Map 3** is called The Rebuild and gives you the chance to rebuild the city yourself.

Download the maps from...
museumoflondon.org.uk/discover/great-fire-1666

GREAT FIRE 1666
EXPERIENCE THE STORY IN MINECRAFT

MUSEUM OF LONDON

PRE-FIRE

1

IT'S 1666

YOU START in a boat on the River Thames and must find your way off. There's a ladder you can climb, explore around the boat until you find it. It's September 1666, the objective is to find 12 audio records to discover what caused the Great Fire of London. Keep your eyes open for maps – these will be essential to complete your mission.

2

KNOW YOUR MAPS

AS YOU explore Old London Town picking up maps you will see that special areas are marked in green. Your location is shown in white. You will also spot landmarks like London Bridge, the river Thames and St Paul's Cathedral (before it had its famous dome). If you find a secret you will get an audio clip of London's history!

3

HEY, IT'S STAMPY!

YOU LEARN as you play in this map. Did you know there were other fires before the Great one? One made London Bridge fall down! You might recognise one of the voices in the audio records you find – it's none other than Stampylongnose himself! The Museum of London did say they had made these maps with Minecraft experts.

4

SPEEDING UP

THE MAPS of old London are huge! So don't be afraid to use the Sprint key to speed up your exploration of the streets. If you go off the map you are holding your direction will be shown by a circle on the map frame. One of the most impressive buildings is St Paul's Cathedral. Walk around the outside until you find a ladder to climb leading up the side.

5

CLIMB A CATHEDRAL

THE LADDERS lead up the side of the building and over the roof and will lead to another audio record telling of a fire that damaged the cathedral. You will find a sketch of the cathedral as you go along. The fire started on Sunday 2nd September in a baker's shop in Pudding Lane. There was lots of rope, hay, coal and tar which helped the fire spread!

6

OFF WITH HER HEAD!

HEAD RIGHT from London Bridge you will find your way to the Tower of London. There are some amazing sailing ships down on the water, see if you can find the famous Traitor's Gate that leads from the water into the tower. This is where traitors of the King were brought inside to meet their deadly fate!

THE FIRE

1

DAY ONE GAME

WHEN YOU start Map 2 you will find yourself inside a museum. There are exhibits all around you that will teach you about Fire Hooks, Water Squirts, Leather Buckets and all the things you will need to help Londoners fight the fire. Then you can start the day one game where you are thrown straight into the action!

2

CAN YOU SMELL BURNING?

YOU'RE IN bed, the flames are already licking around you and you've got to get moving to save yourself, your house and London town! The bells of the churches are ringing to sound the fire alarm! Touch any flame and you'll be set on fire, so you'd better put some of it out! No, don't pull the duvet up and go back to sleep!

3

GRAB AN AXE!

THE TRICK is to use an axe to smash the windows in the top floor of your house. You'll then be able to find the back stairs that will lead out to the street. Now get to Pudding Lane (you can teleport if you find the sign). People will be in shock, wandering the streets. Some of these people have tips for you though, so be sure to stop to chat.

4

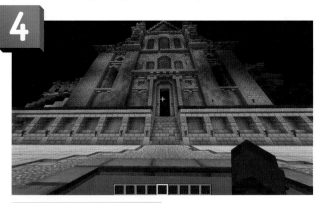

FIND THE CHURCH

FIRE FIGHTING equipment is kept in the church in the centre of the map, so make your way there. You will pass other churches and large buildings that look like churches, but don't be confused. The church you want has large clear glass windows and a large entrance way. No fire brigade existed back in 1666, so the people had to fight the fires.

5

FIRE FIGHTING GEAR

INSIDE THE church you will find a Water Squirt. Grab this, then you need a source of water to make the squirt work. There are sources of water all around the city: troughs, puddles, the river. Hopefully, by exploring London in map one you will have already got an idea of the best places to look for water. Fire hates water.

6

WHERE'S THE WATER?

FILL LEATHER Buckets with water to keep your Water Squirt topped up. All the time you are searching though, the fire will be spreading around the city. The Fire Hook can be used to stop the fire spreading from one building to another, you will see the connecting blocks high above the street – use the hook to pull them down and stop that fire!

26

THE REBUILD

1

LONG LIVE THE KING!

NOW IT'S time to rebuild our capital City. The Museum of London has a third map in their trilogy of Great Fire Minecraft maps. It's called 'The Rebuild'. Start by exploring the ruined streets of London, then you will discover King Charles II at the Guildhall. The King has a vision for a new London, and you can help.

2

FOUR HEADS ARE BETTER THAN ONE

THE MAP has four architects (they're the people who design buildings) for you to interact with: Christopher Wren, Valentine Knight, John Evelyn and Richard Newport. Each of these men had their own unique ideas of how London could be rebuilt. Wide streets, large open squares. Wren was the man who put the dome on St Paul's.

3

52 CHURCHES!

CHRISTOPHER WREN actually built 52 churches around London after the Great Fire. It was the equivalent of Minecraft, only 352 years ago, and using a lot larger blocks. After listening to the four architects you can decide how you would like to rebuild your version of London, using special miniature Minecraft buildings.

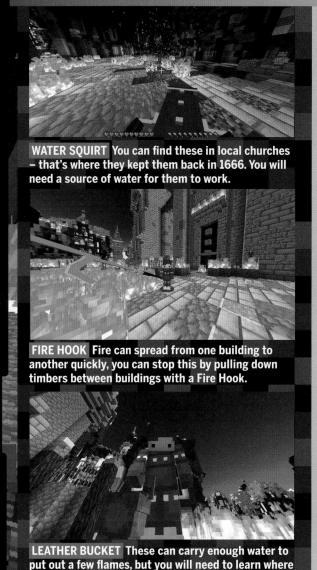

WATER SQUIRT You can find these in local churches – that's where they kept them back in 1666. You will need a source of water for them to work.

FIRE HOOK Fire can spread from one building to another quickly, you can stop this by pulling down timbers between buildings with a Fire Hook.

LEATHER BUCKET These can carry enough water to put out a few flames, but you will need to learn where the puddles and river are to keep topped up!

4

STAR VOICES

YOU WILL get to talk with lots of characters around 'The Rebuild' Minecraft map with voices provided by BigBStaz, NinjaBob, Wizard Keen and even Stampy's dad playing King Charles II! The Museum of London and their Minecraft team have done an excellent job of their Great Fire maps – be sure to download and play them yourself!

Tips

MINECRAFT GLIDE MINI GAME

Top tips on gliding your way around tight corners!

YOU CAN PLAY GLIDE, BATTLE AND TUMBLE ON CONSOLE MINECRAFT!

THE NEED FOR SPEED

WINNING IN Glide on console Minecraft is all about speed! You're dropped right in the deep end, competing against other players around the world, or against your friends. There is a Time Attack mode where the objective is simply to get to the finish line before your competitors, and Score Attack Mode where you must fly through the green rings to earn 3 points –highest score wins! The obvious way of boosting your speed is to fly through the many arrow gates that will give you a short burst – just be sure you don't fly straight into a wall!

PICK A MAP

THERE ARE four maps you can select from in Glide. You start off in Cavern, which is a twisting track through rocky outcrops, Yeti is loads of fun with a giant beast peeking out from icy glaciers, the Kraken map whizzes you past pirate ships where a sea beast awaits, and Dragon gives you a preview of the Chinese Mythology Resource Pack, as you fly past dragons. Each one needs lightning reflexes if you are to stand any chance of winning – take a few goes to learn the route by playing Solo before you can expect to be placing high on the multiplayer leaderboard.

REACH FOR THE SKIES

SUCCESSFULLY RACING around each map will rely on you being at the correct height for important twists and turns. Keep an eye open for the fiery square pools with steam coming off them. This steam will push you up in the air, giving you new height that you can use to survey the area before swooping down.

1 seconds to reach the end!

REAR VIEW MIRROR

WANT TO find out who is on your tail? Well luckily there's a 'Look Behind' button that will give you a quick glimpse, which can be very useful in Time Attack Mode. If they are following closely behind you because you know where you're going and they don't, try to lead them towards a trap! A cliff face will do, just dart to the side at the last minute and laugh as they splat into the rocks. It's also useful to look behind on the finish line if you're in first place – there might be someone coming up fast!

CUT THE CORNER

STILL NOT managing to win? We bet you're missing out on all the shortcuts that have been hidden away throughout the maps. A good plan would be to spend some time playing the game in Solo mode again where you can go slowly and explore the walls and hidden areas to familiarise yourself with the shortcuts. Some are really tiny gaps and you will need to be highly accurate to make it through without bashing your head!

HANG ON... LET ME JUST DRINK THIS POTION BEFORE WE FIGHT!

MINECRAFT BATTLE MINI GAME

The winner is the last one standing, can you survive?

BEAT THAT CHEST

BATTLE IS a kind of Hunger Games where you've got to attack anyone and everyone you come across. Be sure to check out the contents of every Chest you discover – they will have armour, food, weapons and potions to help you.

POTION POWER

THERE ARE negative and positive Potions found in Chests. In one-on-one combat, you will gain a big advantage over your foe if you throw a negative potion at them, doing more damage than a sword swipe alone. Be sure to take a positive one before a battle, as well as munching a few apples to increase your hunger bar.

CROWDED BATTLES

UP TO 16 players can now battle it out simultaneously in Battle, which makes for some frantic games! The maps don't get any bigger, and there are no extra Chests, so when you are all facing off against each other at the start jump into the Chests if you are confident on getting there before someone else, or a good tactic is just to run away in the opposite direction! Chests refill over time, so you can always come back later. Pushing people from a high height is an effective way of causing them damage. If you see someone falling from a height, a few swipes with a weapon could just finish them off.

GRAB THEIR STUFF!

WHEN YOU manage to kill someone they will drop all of their stuff, which is then ripe for picking up! To start with you need to concentrate on defending yourself, keeping out of the way of other players while you stock up on essential armour, weapons, potions and food. Once you are confident you have some great stuff in your inventory you can then go on the hunt – taking players out with a clever combination of throwing potions and attacking, while wearing some good armour.

MINECRAFT
CONSOLE EDITION
TUMBLE MINI GAME

Shovels or snowballs – time for some Tumble!

RoRoJnRi

DIG FOR VICTORY

THERE ARE two styles of gameplay in Tumble, one where everyone has a Shovel and must dig the blocks from underneath enemies, the other is Snowballs, which we will come to in a bit. Shovels is certainly the toughest mode as it is close up gameplay. One important thing to avoid is Soul Sand – these brown blocks will slow you down making you an easy target! If you spot two players having a bit of a fight, creep up behind one of them and dig the block underneath them away before they know you're even there! If you're good at parkour, you'll be at an advantage here!

ICY MOVES

YOU NEED to use slightly different tactics to win in a Snowball game. These icy weapons can be used close up or from a distance and the trick is to aim at the other player's feet, trying to smash the block they are just about to walk on to. The Snowballs are unlimited and fly through the air in an arc, so aim higher than the enemy to knock them off a ledge. A great tactic is to climb up to the top layers in the map, make a hole in the ground and fire hundreds of Snowballs through the hole at the players below!

SKIN PACK FUN

THE MINI GAME MASTERS SKIN PACK was released to celebrate Glide going live on PS4 and Xbox One. It's full of super sporting skins that look great when you're gliding around the tricky maps in Glide, battling for your life in Battle or tumbling off ledges in Tumble. The skins are split into teams – Team Creeper, Team Guardian and Team Zombie to name just a few, with all kinds of weird combinations going on (chicken on the head, anyone?). As ever, you can sample some of these skins for free, but for the full pack you will need to spend £1.69. Be sure to ask a grown-up before making in-game purchases.

TRICKY TROPHIES

THERE ARE trophies you can achieve if you complete set challenges in the game. For example, you can get a 'S-No Throw' if you win a game without throwing a single Snowball. A very tricky achievement indeed. To get this one you'll have to run around avoiding other players while they battle it out with each other, then knock the blocks from underneath the final enemy with your fists. Attack the same player with 25 Snowballs in a single round and you will get 'Snow Storm', and we also got a 'Hotshot' trophy for landing a Snowball on someone while we fell into the lava – aaarrrgggghhh!

SPECTATOR SPORT

IN BOTH Battle and Tumble, once you die you turn into a bat and can fly around the map checking out all the cool stuff. This is a great way of familiarising yourself with the various types of terrain before you jump back into another game. In such fast and frantic mini-games, taking your time as a Bat can be a welcome break!

I PREFER TO PLAY WITH SHOVELS RATHER THAN SNOWBALLS!

40 MINUTES!

HOW MANY TICKLES DOES IT TAKE TO MAKE A SQUID LAUGH? TEN-TICKLES!

A SEA MONSTER

A saltwater monstrous fright for you all... aarrgh!

DIFFICULTY

NORMAL
THERE'S SOME TRICKY DETAIL IN THIS BUILD, BUT YOU CAN DO IT!

START HERE!

1 FIRST ADD Blue Wool, White Wool, Red Wool, and Nether Wart block to your hotbar. Next create a forked tongue out of Nether Wart – each of the main lengths behind the front of the tongue are 3, 3, 4 and 4. From here, create a step structure from Blue Wool and add in the White and Red as shown.

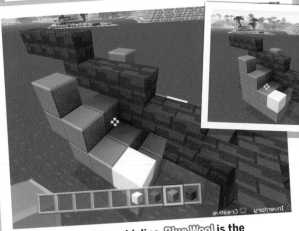

2 AS A quick guideline, Blue Wool is the monster's skin, White are the teeth, and Red is used for the mouth. Got it? Cool. Let's move on. Head round to the other side of the tongue and mirror what we just made before filling in the lower Blue Wool sections.

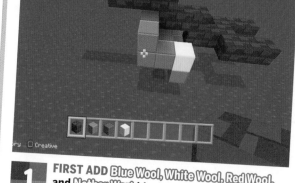

3 NOW WE'LL get to work on the monster's mouth. At the top-back of what will be the lower jaw, place 1 Red Wool diagonally, then a row of 2 diagonally from that. On the underside of the last section of the tongue, go 1 block down and extend the Red Wool out.

4 ADD 2 long diagonal rows at the back, and on the 2 rows from Step 3, turn the 2 into a square of 4 then drop a block behind each side. Build a 5-high frame at the back, extend it out so it's 2 blocks in depth, fill in the back, and finish with 3 diagonal rows heading forward.

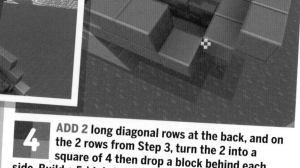

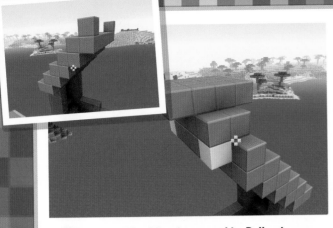

5 **BACK TO** adding in some skin. Pull out your Blue Wool once more and run a zig-zag (Tetris block!) formation along the side of the Red Wool. Add 2 blocks on both sides of the top. In between those blocks, build a platform coming off, with 2 more teeth, and a smaller platform on top.

6 **BY NOW** your monster should be starting to take shape, so let's begin work on the rest of the head. Go back down to the back-middle of the jaw. From here, build the skin area away from the zig-zags. You should be able to connect this section down so it feeds into the lower jaw.

7 **NEXT COMES** the head and eyes. For this, grab Black Wool and an eye colour (we used Lime Wool). But before you lay down the eyes, use Blue Wool to build the front section by the teeth down the middle of the head. On the last section, that's where you can add in the eyes.

8 **THIS NEXT** one is nice and simple. At the back of the head, create an oval shape. The dimensions for this are 4 on the left and right sides, 4 single blocks heading inward above and below, then 2 3-long rows at the top and bottom to connect it all together.

9 **NOW COMES** the last part of the head. From the 2 3-long rows, add more rows 1 block away so it connects into the head. Do this again on the bottom as well. You should be left with a few gaps either side so go ahead and patch them up with more Blue Wool.

10 **FOR THE** first section of the body, go back to the oval shape. Make a mental note of the dimensions from Step 8, then begin building the shape out so it's 10 blocks in length. You can make it longer if you want a bigger Sea Monster, but for now, stick with 10.

11 TO ADD some curves into the blue beast, you have to first rebuild the oval shape, only this time build it 1 block down. Extend this new section out for a total of 4 blocks in length. Then, at the back of the body, build another oval shape 1 block down from that.

12 AS YOU can see from the image above, the goal now is to build the body out until you reach the Water below. For this, just keep creating oval shapes, extending them, and moving each section down by 1 block. When you're a few blocks underwater, stop building.

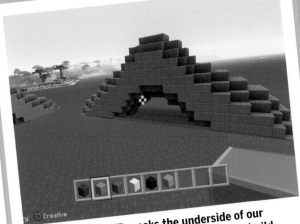

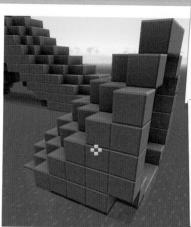

13 THE WATER masks the underside of our monster, meaning you don't need to build anything underwater. Handy, right? Next up, head to the right of big blue, and start building an oval from underwater. Continue this up, then when it's high enough, build it back down to Water level.

14 FOR THE tail, just build another oval coming out of the Water like in the last step, only when you get to the point where the oval isn't submerged, build a flat section coming from the upper half. From here, you should be able to connect the bottom upwards towards the flat bit.

15 FEEL FREE to go ahead and make ol' bitey's teeth much larger (and sharper!). For our last section of this Sea Monster build, make a 3-wide small wing on the left side out of Blue Wool and Light Blue Wool. Do the same on the opposite side and that's this build complete! It's a monster... arrrrrghhhh!

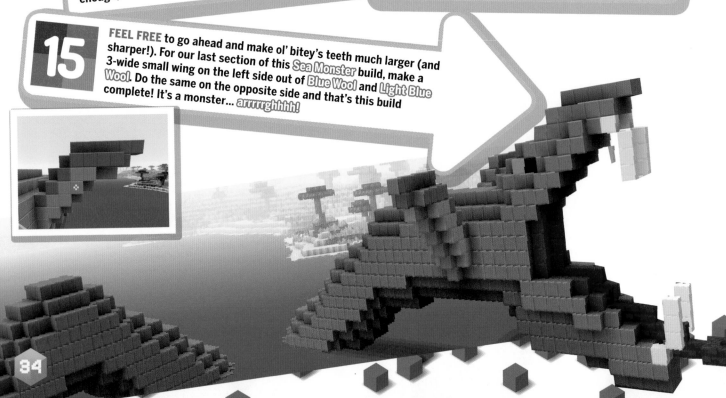

PUZZLES

Test your brains with these teasers...

TRICKY CROSSING

STEVE HAS to get a Wolf, a Chicken and a loaf of Bread from one side of the river to the other. He has crafted a Boat, but it's only big enough to carry himself and one other thing. The problem is that if the wolf and chicken are left behind, the Wolf will eat the Chicken. If the Chicken and Bread are left together, there will be no bread left when Steve returns. How can he get all three of them to the other side of the river?

I WISH THEY WOULD HURRY UP AND CROSS – I WANT TO SWIM HOME

ANSWERS ON PAGE 93

HOW MANY BLOCKS?

THIS ONE will test your Minecraft block skills. How many blocks do you think there are in this build below? We made it from a solid 4x4x4 block and if you can't see the block, it is there. Count them up!

WRITE IN HOW MANY YOU THINK!

FIND THE WORD

WE HAVE hidden a well-used Minecraft block in this 3x3 grid of letters. By tracing a line from the first letter to the last, only going up, down, left or right, can you work out which block is hiding here?

N	D	S
A	S	T
A	E	N	O

CUTE DOG!

An easy dog in four simple steps... woof!

SQUIRREL!

5 MINUTES!

START HERE!

1 OUR CUTE dog is a lovely simple build for Minecraft beginners. He has a 5x5 Oak Wood block body with legs placed at the 4 corners, longer at the front than at the back. We've used Glowstone blocks for his paws and extended out by 1 block with a 3x3 block area to make a snout on one side.

2 HIS EARS are made from Glowstone blocks followed by Oak Wood blocks again – sticking out either side of his body. We have turned one of the Wooden blocks on his snout into a Black Wool block nose and added a tail at the back, again with Glowstone and Oak Wood blocks.

DIFFICULTY

EASY
WE'LL HAVE THIS DOG SITTING UP AND BEGGING IN NO TIME!

3 NOW FOR the dog's eyes – build up on top of the ear blocks you already placed to give a line of Oak Wood, White Wool and Black Wool blocks to create his Minecraft-style eyes. Hooray – now he can see where he's going!

BUILD THIS!

4 ALL THAT is left to do is add the final line of Oak Wood blocks on top of his eyes to complete the dog's face. Don't you think he's cute? Well actually, built in the sand he looks like an Egyptian Sphinx! If you want to make a dog that looks like your own pet – just change the Oak Wood to something that looks like your dog's colour!

Make it!
MOB BALLOONS!

MOB PARTY BALLOONS!

TIME NEEDED: 10 MINUTES
EXTRA INFO: WE'VE SHOWN YOU 3 – BUT THINK ABOUT OTHERS YOU COULD MAKE!

YOU'LL NEED...

ITEMS: Coloured balloons – mainly round, but you could try the long ones too. Thick black marker pen and Tipex-style correction fluid or white paint!

DIFFICULTY

EASY
A FANTASTIC WAY TO THEME A PARTY WITH MINECRAFT MOBS!

1 CRAFTY CREEPERS

MAKING MINECRAFT party balloons for your next birthday bash is not only easy, it's great fun to do too! There are many companies that will sell you these, but we say "Make your own!". Firstly, take a green regular round balloon and inflate it. It takes a lot of puff, so you might want your grown-up helper to do this for you – they're full of wind! With a nicely inflated and tied balloon, take the thick black marker pen and draw on the Creeper face – just the same as we have here. It's simply made of two squares for eyes, a rectangle for a nose and mouth then the square fangs. You know what a Creeper looks like – draw it on!

CREEPERS WORK REALLY WELL ON BALLOONS!

2 THE FACE OF A PIG!

YOU NEED a nice pink balloon next – we're going to do the pig! Again, blow up the balloon so it's easy to draw on, then add two black squares for his eyeballs, and then put two white squares next to these for the whites of his eyes, using your correction fluid or white paint. Then two more black squares for his nose, finishing off with a rectangle of white around his nose. Check out our balloon here if you're not sure where to put the markings.

3 BLOW 'EM UP!

AS WE'RE blowing things up, why not make a TNT Block to go with your two mobs? Take a red balloon and make a white rectangle in the centre. Now, carefully draw on the TNT letters, but do it in a Minecraft-style pixel way like we have here. You can keep on going with your pack of coloured balloons – a white one makes a great Ghast, a black one could be an Enderman, with a bit of colouring in for the eyes. Can you think of any others?

CAN YOU THINK OF OTHER MOBS THAT WOULD WORK?

HOW TO DEFEAT CREEPERS

Our Minecraft Experts show you the best way...

▶ IN YOUR SIGHTS

BLAMMO! The safest way to dispatch Creepers is always going to be arrows. Using a bow means you'll have distance between you and the Creeper, so there's no chance of it exploding. Also, if you don't have a bow, getting a Skeleton to shoot the Creeper results in a mob battle to the death!

▶ WET MOB!

SOGGINESS RULES! Creepers do absolutely no damage in water. This is your biggest strength when battling them. If you see a Creeper, lure it into a nearby water source. It'll still blow up when you whack it, but the water absorbs the impact, leaving you damage-free. Just be careful they don't climb onto a block and explode.

▶ SWORD PLAY

BE WARNED Swords are surely the least safest way to attack Creepers. That said, there is a way to use Swords without insta-dying. The tactic here is to sprint at the Creeper, hit it twice, then back away. The Creeper will start flashing, but backing off calms it down. Then just repeat this step until it finally drops.

▶ MOGGY MOBS!

MEOW! ARGH! Who's scared of cats? Creepers, that's who. For some reason they can't stand Ocelots. When they see an Ocelot, they run in the opposite direction, making Ocelots a great home defence. Or better yet, attach one to a lead and you'll stay Creeper-free while exploring all you like.

BOOM BOOM!

EXPLOSIONS ARE annoying, right? But what about if we're the ones doing the exploding? To create a landmine, place TNT into the ground with a block above it, then a pressure plate on the block. When the Creeper walks over it, they'll get a taste of their own medicine.

OVER THE TOP!

EVERYTHING IN Minecraft causes knockback, and we can use that to our advantage. When underground, or near a cliff, the easiest way to stop Creepers is to line them up, then poke them off the edge of something high. If it's high enough, the fall damage will end them.

PIT STOP

HERE'S A thought: you can always create a handy Creeper pit in front of your property, permanently securing the place. For this, just dig out a 7 deep, however-long trench, and when the Creepers fall in, you can pick them off with Arrows or even a Fishing Rod to cause fall damage.

I AM A MOLE...

HOLY SMOKE! If you've got a Creeper's attention, dig a 3 block deep hole and line it up so the Creeper falls into it. When it does, back off so it doesn't explode, and when it's back to normal, run in and cover the hole over. Now run away and the Creeper should eventually despawn.

HOT STUFF!

LAVA LAVA pants on fire! When you see a Creeper, dunk a Bucket of Lava at its feet. Better yet, if you can get above the Creeper, drop the Lava off the side and you won't need to run for your life. Quick, easy, and totally safe. Just don't stand in the Lava, yeah?

SHINE A LIGHT

ALWAYS REMEMBER a light source means mobs can't spawn. Creepers can spawn at any time of the day, but not where there is a light source. So that's Torches, Sea Lanterns, Glowstone, Lava, and even Ender-Rods. Deck your home out in a bazillion torches and it'll be Creeper-free for life!

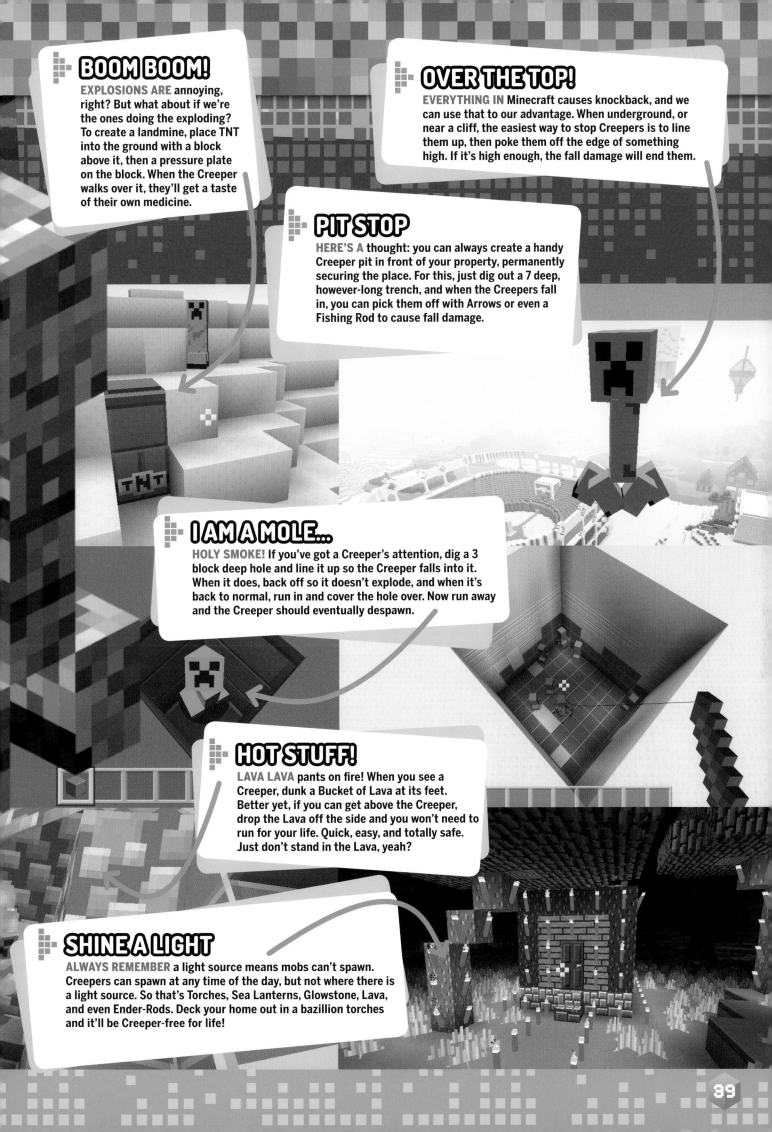

Build

DIFFICULTY

★★★

HARD
REDSTONE IS TRICKY STUFF, YOU NEED TO FOLLOW CLOSELY!

1 HOUR 45 MINS

BEFORE – JUST A REGULAR FIREPLACE?

AFTER – OPENS TO A SECRET ROOM!

SECRET FIREPLACE

TIME NEEDED: 1 HOUR 45 MINS
EXTRA INFO: THIS IS A GOOD BUILD TO DO BEFORE YOU BUILD A MANSION HOUSE

INFO

BUILD A SECRET FIREPLACE

Hide a special room behind the fireplace in a Minecraft house using Redstone!

THE POWER OF FIRE WILL ALWAYS AMAZE! THIS ONE TURNS INTO A DOORWAY!

MINECRAFT GETS really tricky when you start messing around with Redstone! Think of it like an electrical circuit that you can wire up to do whatever you want. In this build we show you how to use the different blocks of Redstone to create a fireplace in your house that will move to one side, revealing the entrance to a secret room where you can store your most precious posessions! Let's get building...

1

CLEAR THE WAY

START OFF by finding a nice, big open area in your world to start your build (remember it's quicker to burn down trees and use Water Buckets to clear away shrubs). Next, build a big old 12x6 hole that's 2 blocks deep.

2
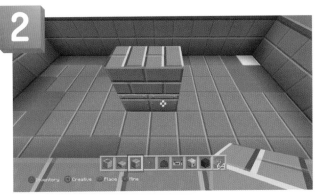

LOAD UP YOUR HOTBAR

ADD A Stone Brick, Stone Half Slab, Sticky Piston, Redstone Torch, Redstone Dust, Redstone Repeater, Dispenser, Netherbrick, and Fire Charges to your hotbar. Then place 2 Sticky Pistons facing up with Stone Bricks on top.

3

CHECK YOUR REDSTONE

IT'S WORTH mentioning here before we go on, with Redstone builds it's important you triple check everything. With that in mind, 1 block diagonally behind the Sticky Pistons place 2 blocks of Stone Bricks with a Redstone Torch on each.

4
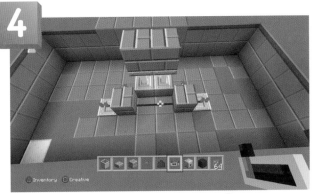

AROUND THE BACK

HEAD AROUND the back of the build. On the left hand side, place a Redstone Repeater facing outward. Do the same for the block on the right. Then with Redstone Dust, run a line of 2 in-between the blocks.

5

LINE IT UP

GET YOUR Stone Bricks out again and place 1 block of Stone Brick on the far left, next to the Repeater. Next place a Stone Brick block on the far right side. At this point everything should be lining up symmetrically.

6
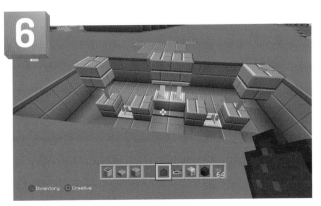

BALANCING TORCHES

ON EACH of the 2 blocks you placed, put a Redstone Torch directly on top. Then on top of the Torches, place a single Stone Brick. To finish, grab your Redstone Dust and drop a piece on top of each new block.

7

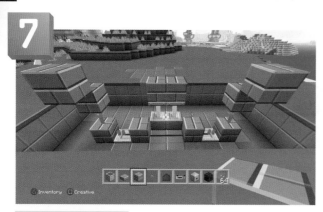

MORE BRICKS

THIS NEXT part of the build is nice and simple. Diagonally up and 1 block out from the blocks with **Redstone Dust** on, place in another **Stone Brick** coming off on both sides. And remember, it's all got to be symmetrical.

8

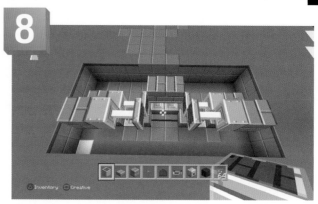

STICKY PISTON FUN

NOW WE'RE going to add in some **Sticky Pistons**, 4 to be exact. On the inside of the last 2 blocks you placed, add an inward facing **Sticky Piston**. Then add 2 more on the **Redstone Dust** blocks, again, facing inward.

9

ADD FIRE CHARGES

GO AROUND to the front side of the contraption you're building. Everything still symmetrical? Good. On top of each of the lower **Sticky Pistons**, place **2 Dispensers** on either side facing inward, and fill them with **Fire Charges**.

10

USING NETHERBRICKS

PLACE NETHERBRICK in-between both of the extended lower **Pistons**. Go 1 block up from there and place 2 blocks behind and 1 on both sides (the blocks on the side carry the **Fire Charge** needed for relighting the fire).

11

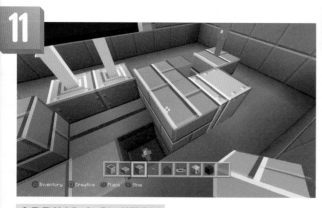

ADDING A SWITCH

THAT'S THE main bulk of this section out the way. For our on/off switch, head to the base of the structure. Put a **Brick** coming off the block with a **Torch** on, then place a **Sticky Piston** behind it, and a **Redstone Torch** in the floor.

12

MORE WIRING UP

BEHIND THE Sticky Piston, place down a **Repeater** going into it. Then behind the Repeater place a regular **Piston** 1 block into the floor. And finally, place 1 block of **Sand** on top of the Piston. We're almost there now!

13

REPEATERS... REPEATING

PLACE 3 blocks of Stone Bricks forming a reverse 'L' shape behind the Sand block. So it's like a mini step. On top of the first block, drop down a Redstone Repeater. On the block 1 up from that, dust it with Redstone.

14

TEST THE OPENING

DROP A block above the Dust and put a Button on its face. You should now be able to press the Button and watch as your Fireplace magically opens. Press the Button again and it'll close and relight itself. Pretty cool, right?

15

BUILD THE FIREPLACE

REPLACE THE Button Stone with Grey Glazed Terracotta to look like wallpaper. Then run 2 more next to it, count 4 blocks, then add another 3. In the centre, begin to make what will become our fireplace surround.

REDSTONE TIPS

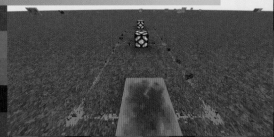

THERE ARE lots of ways you can obtain Redstone. Mine some Redstone Ore, smelt it down using any fuel you like, smashing Jungle traps, killing a witch, trading it with Villagers or gathering up Redstone Dust that has been placed before will all gather up the good stuff. You can break Redstone with pretty much anything from your fists to the best weapons.

BREWING, CRAFTING and circuits all use Redstone in one way or another. For example, making a Mundane Potion is done with Redstone and a Water Bottle. Mundane Potions are then used to go on and create more exciting Potions! Then crafting many potions with Redstone will increase their duration, although with some it will decrease the level.

MANY OBJECTS need Redstone in their Crafting ingredients to work. A Clock is made with Redstone and 4 blocks of Gold, a Compass is Redstone and 4 blocks of Iron Ingot and a Piston is Redstone with 3 Wood Planks, 4 Cobblestone and an Iron Ingot. Then there are all the Redstone bits – a Redstone Torch, for example, is made from Redstone and a Stick.

WHEN MAKING Redstone circuits, it's important to know that the power Redstone Dust can carry gets weaker the further away from the power source it goes. The maximum distance is 15 blocks. If you need to go further than this you will have to incorporate Redstone Repeaters into your circuit that will boost the power level back up to 15.

16

MORE REDSTONE WIRING

FOR THE inside Button. Place a second Redstone Torch in the centre at the bottom next to the other, a Repeater in front of the right-side block, and a dusted block behind the Repeater. Lastly, drop a block above the Dust with a Button on.

17

MAKING WALLS

NOW HEAD back to the front of the contraption and build a walkway going through the middle. Build the glazed Terracotta walls up, change the floor for Wooden Planks, and then create a fireplace out of Stone Bricks and Stone Steps.

18

THE SECRET ROOM

BUT WHERE does the fireplace lead to? How about adding a spiral door with a secret room? Head to the end of the walkway and dig a 5 deep, 7x6 hole. Place Stone Bricks in the formation seen in the image.

19

A SPIRAL EFFECT

HEAD TO the other side of the would-be-door. Now with Sticky Pistons, place 4 as they are in the image above. The blocks they're attached to will be the blocks that move to create a spiral effect and wow your friends!

20

MORE STONE BRICKS

GO BACK around the front of the fire and look at the Piston that is now on your left. Drop a Stone Brick below it, and 1 block diagonally underneath. The gap behind the last block is where you go for the next step.

21

PLACING PISTONS

BELOW THE first Stone Brick from Step 20, place a downward Sticky Piston with a block of Redstone below it, a Repeater to the right, a Stone Brick to the right of that, then another Sticky Piston facing up on top of the Brick.

22

IS REDSTONE WEIRD?

BEHIND THE Stone Brick on the right, create an 'L' out of Redstone Dust leading into another brick with a Redstone Torch on. Above that Torch, place yet another block with another Redstone Torch on. Yes, Redstone IS weird.

23

WATCH YOUR TICKS

PLACE A block with Redstone Dust on it above the Redstone Torch. Drop a block to the left with a West-facing, 2-tick Repeater on. To finish this step, drop some more Redstone Dust on the block to the left.

24

NEARLY THERE...

LOOK AT the front of the door. On the Western 2 blocks, add a single Stone Brick on the upper side. Place a Redstone Torch underneath on the wall, then a Button on the opposite side of the block and you're all finished!

25

WHAT WILL YOU HIDE?

YOU CAN build whatever you want on the other side of the door. If you've got lots of epic loot you don't want people messing with, this is a great place to keep it. But we think that Iron blocks make for a great little bank vault!

26

DECORATE YOUR ROOM

TO ROUND this build out, bring your walls back round onto themselves, add in a Door, decorate the floor with a nice Carpet and add in Windows. Now go forth and amaze your friends with the greatest secret fireplace room they've ever seen!

YOUR FRIENDS WILL BE AMAZED WHEN YOU SHOW THEM THE SECRET ROOM BEHIND THE FIRE!

Make it!
TNT BLOCK PIZZA!

DIFFICULTY

EASY
THESE PIZZAS ARE REALLY EASY TO MAKE, BUT LOOK GREAT!

Turn teatime into an explosive success with our TNT block pizza recipe. These fiery blocks are great for Minecraft parties too!

INFO

TNT BLOCK PIZZA

TIME NEEDED: 30 MINUTES
EXTRA INFO: IF YOU SHOP AROUND YOU CAN EVEN FIND SQUARE PIZZA BASES!

YOU'LL NEED...

INGREDIENTS: Ready made pizza bases (round or square), pepperoni slices, pizza topping sauce, black olives, your favourite cheese (mozzarella works well)
PREPARATION: Wash your hands!

1 TRIMMING

SO YOU'RE already drooling at the thought of eating a Minecraft TNT Block Pizza, aren't you? If you're lucky, you can actually find square pizza bases for sale in the supermarket. Or there are really posh ones from celebrity chefs that you can roll out and use. If you're not so lucky then don't worry... you can take a regular circular pizza base and cut off the edges (ask a grown up to help you with sharp knives). You will need to make sure you end up with a nice square pizza base, like our one here...

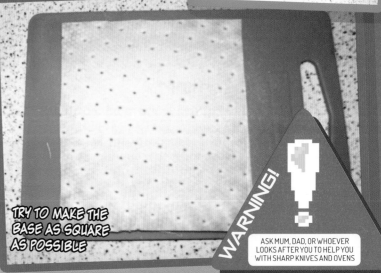

TRY TO MAKE THE BASE AS SQUARE AS POSSIBLE

WARNING!
ASK MUM, DAD, OR WHOEVER LOOKS AFTER YOU TO HELP YOU WITH SHARP KNIVES AND OVENS

IF YOU CAN'T GET PIZZA SAUCE - KETCHUP IS A GOOD ALTERNATIVE!

2 SAUCY

WE'RE MAKING two pizzas at the same time with different cheeses. For each one you need to use a teaspoon to spoon out a dollop of tomato pizza sauce into the centre of your square base, then spread it all around. The important thing here is to make sure you cover every corner of the base, and all the way to the edges. No one likes a piece of pizza with no sauce on it! Don't worry if you get a bit messy on this bit – just lick the sauce off your fingers. (You did remember to wash your hands, right?)

3 HOT STUFF

YOUR TNT block is split into three horizontal rectangle shapes – two of red, one of white (well OK, yellow, depending on the type of cheese you use). To make the red areas of the TNT Block you need to take your pepperoni slices and line them from one side of the pizza to the other, taking care to overlap the slices to give a solid colour with no gaps. Ask your grown up to help you cut some of the slices in half so that you can have a nice straight line. Repeat this for the bottom part of your TNT Block pizza, leaving a gap for cheese.

4 A BAND OF CHEESE

WE'VE HEARD a few cheesey bands in our time, but this one wins hands down! Take your cheese and cut it into slices, if it's not already. Here we have chosen the traditional pizza cheese mozzarella as it gives a wonderfully gooey finished result, but as you can see it doesn't slice very well. The main thing is to make sure you fill in all the gap through the centre of your TNT Block. When the cheese melts in the oven it will form one gooey band of colour.

OH LOOK! PAC-MAN PEPPERONI!

YOU CAN ALWAYS USE PEPPERS INSTEAD OF PEPPERONI... SOB!

MAKE SURE YOUR PIZZA IS COVERED!

5 LETTERS

NOW TO write 'TNT' across your pizza for that TNT Block finishing touch. Drain your olives from their jar and use a blunt knife (for safety, of course!) to cut them into halves. If your olives are quite big, you can cut them into quarters. Now you can think of each piece of olive as a 'pixel' and write 'TNT' in olives. The trick is to start in the centre with the letter 'N'. That way you will know that your letters will be bang on the centre of your pizza. Add in the two 'T's either side and you're done!

OLIVE PIXELS ARE GREAT FUN!

FINISHED!

POP YOUR TNT Block pizza into a preheated oven at 180°C for around 20 minutes. Just enough time for the cheese to melt into a lovely gooey band across your block. Make sure you watch your pizzas cook though – the pepperoni can start to burn easily as it's not got cheese on top. Yum! Tuck in.

Tips

SKINS

This works on...
- [×] Computer Edition
- [ ] Pocket Edition
- [ ] Console Edition

STEVE AND Alex are great, but personalising your skin is the first thing you should do to customise your game. On computers you upload a new skin file to your Minecraft.net profile page. On console you can choose from 16 default skins, or buy a Skin Pack like the recent Power Rangers one. On Pocket Edition, Skin Packs can also be bought as in-app purchases, or you can download skin files to your photo library then upload these to the game. Remember to ask a grown up before purchasing anything online.

WE LOVE THIS TAZMANIAN DEVIL SKIN - THEY'VE USED THE BODY TO MAKE HIS MOUTH LOOK EXTRA BIG!

THERE ARE 1,000s OF SKINS TO DOWNLOAD - LOOK! IT'S ROBBIE ROTTEN FROM LAZY TOWN!

STILL PLAYING VANILLA MINECRAFT? THERE'S SO MUCH MORE YOU CAN DO...

CUSTOMISING MINECRAFT

The noob's guide to making Minecraft your own!

MODS

This works on...
- [×] Computer Edition

TAKING MINECRAFT to the next level are the Mods. These files change the game in big ways. There are too many to list here, but the ones we like the best are those that add cool content – Mo' Creatures adds in 79 new animals to the game which is brilliant fun, you can find it at mocreatures.org. Galacticraft adds rockets and space stuff to the inventory – place a rocket on a launch pad and you can travel to planets all over the galaxy – it's so epic! These two need an installer program called Forge installed first. This handles all the tricky placing of files for you. It's quite safe, and instructions can be found at files.minecraftforge. There are lots of YouTube videos that show you the best Mods and how to install them. Have fun!

ROBBIE, HOLDING A ROCKET, SURROUNDED BY KOMODO DRAGONS. ONLY POSSIBLE WITH MOBS!

IN GALACTICRAFT YOU CAN BUILD ROCKETS, THEN JUMP IN TO FLY OFF TO DISTANT PLANETS! LOOK - ROBBIE ROTTEN IS ON MARS!

RESOURCE PACKS

This works on...
Computer Edition
Pocket Edition
Console Edition

WHEN TEXTURES, 3D models, music, sound effects and fonts are all customised together, it's called a Resource Pack. Have you seen those Minecraft pictures with super-realistic water and clouds? That's a Resource Pack in action. On Console Minecraft they call them Mash-Up packs. Some of the best we've seen are the Super Mario Edition on Wii-U, downloadable from the Nintendo eShop, and the new Adventure Time mash-up for all consoles. Pocket Edition mash-ups on Android devices can be downloaded, on Apple devices you must buy them as in-app purchases.

RESOURCES...

A GOOD place to start is Minecraft.net – it's the central place for everything Minecraft, especially the new Pocket and Windows 10 Add-Ons. We also love planetminecraft.com. A great website run by the Minecraft community packed with skins, texture packs and mods.

ADD-ONS

This works on...
Pocket Edition

3D MODELS, textures and behaviours of mobs can be played with using the Add-Ons that Mojang is currently trialling on Pocket and Windows 10 Edition. Want a Creeper that is the height of a house? You got it! Want Pigs that explode on touch? Why not? When you've made something really cool, you can then share it with your friends on Minecraft Realms too. Once fully tested, we expect to see Add-Ons on all versions of the game.

THIS ADD-ON IS CALLED 'ALIEN INVASION'. IT WAS USED BY MOJANG TO DEMO ADD-ONS AT THE BIG E3 COMPUTER GAMES SHOW IN AMERICA.

EVERYONE WHO WENT TO MINECON 2016 GOT TO DOWNLOAD THIS SPECIAL CAPE WITH AN ENDERMAN'S EYES ON IT!

CAPES

This works on...
Computer Edition
Console Edition

YOU'VE GOT to be really special to earn yourself a cape in Minecraft! Just like a super hero, it's a special extra item of clothing that not everyone can have. All Mojang staff have special capes with the company logo on them, and players lucky enough to attend the MineCon events could download capes too on both the Computer and Xbox Editions. If you just want to wear a Cape for fun, you can use a Mod like the one at MinecraftCapes.co.uk that will allow you to customise your own – like our 'M' cape here!

THE MEGA MEAT MACHINE!

WAIT A MINUTE... I DON'T LIKE THE SOUND OF THIS BUILD!

Your favourite meat at the touch of a button!

30 MINUTES!

START HERE!

GATHER THIS STUFF!

DIFFICULTY

HARD
THIS BUILD USES COMPLICATED REDSTONE FEATURES

1 FEELING HUNGRY? This hard build project is a Mega Meat Machine! We're showing you how to make a vending machine for meat using tricky Redstone. First of all make a 7x3x1 box out of the block of your choice, then knock 3 holes in it and fill with a contrasting block, with 3 buttons on top.

2 ON THE back of your vending machine box put 3 Redstone Torches on the 3 contrasting blocks. Now you need to dig a giant hole underneath this mega machine for all the Redstone circuits we're going to add later. It should be 7x5 and 2 blocks deep.

3 PLACE THREE Wool blocks behind the machine, up against the outer wall, with 1 block gaps between them. On top of these place 3 Hoppers for each Wool block, but Crouch while placing them so they lead into the block below them. Finally place a Chest on top of each Hopper stack.

4 BREAK TWO of the Wool blocks, leaving the furthest right one. Now place a Hopper while looking at the side of the Wool block, then a further 3 Hoppers leading into the first one, but place these while Crouching otherwise you will open the Hopper, not place it leading into the next one.

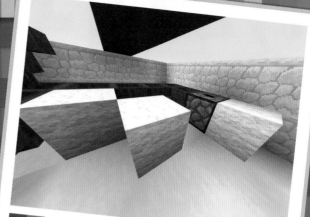

5 NOW GO to the front of the machine. You need to place a Dropper facing up in the centre of the wall, then place 6 more Hoppers leading into the Dropper, for the final one you will have to break the remaining Wool block. Remember – you need to be Crouching while placing them for this to work.

6 TIME TO get those Wool blocks back out again! Place one next to the Dropper, one in the corner created by the Hoppers, and the final one, 1 block away from the Dropper (as you can see in the picture above). These will be used for taking Redstone signals around your machine!

7 HERE COMES the complicated part! Place a Comparator (it looks like a triangle!) between the Dropper and the Wool block, facing into the Wool block. Next, place 2 Repeaters, one facing into the Wool block next to the Dropper, the other one facing out from the Wool block in the corner next to the Hoppers.

8 TIME FOR some Redstone fun! Place 2 Redstone Dust on the ground – one next to each Repeater. Then a third behind the Wool block, as shown above. With that done, fill the 3 Chests placed earlier with 3 types of your favourite meat – one type of meat in each Chest. Mmm... pork chops.

9 YOU NOW must fill in the hole in front of your machine to hide the mechanics, but be sure not to click any of the Redstone while you do as your machine will break down! On the front, place 3 Item Frames with your meat choices in each Frame to show people which button to press. Now, pressing a button delivers some meat!

WOW! I THINK EVERY SHOP SHOULD HAVE A MEAT MACHINE!

BUILD THIS!

Meat Machine!

PUZZLES

Test your brains with these teasers...

YUM... ARE THERE ANY FLIES FOR ME?

SCOFF TIME!

WE ALL KNOW what kind of foods these 5 animals love in Minecraft, but this lunchtime they have decided to try something new. Can you work out which food each animal is scoffing? Follow the lines and all will be revealed!

TRACKBLOCKS

UNRAVEL THE three nine-letter Minecraft-related words on each face of each block. Ready, set... go!

WOAH! THIS IS LIKE 3 PUZZLES IN 1! GOOD LUCK!

O G L
O N T O W
N E S W
O N O H S C
S S H F I L
I U U N W O
O P

MYSTERY MOB CRISS-CROSS

THERE'S A mob hiding out inside this criss-cross puzzle, and it's your job to find them! Answer all the super-tricky Minecraft clues, slot the words into the puzzle, then look for the highlighted letters. They will spell out the name of the mystery mob – only the letters will be scrambled. Can you catch them? You will find all the answers on page 93.

ANSWERS ON PAGE **93**

CAN YOU FIND ALL THE MINECRAFT ANSWERS?

FILL IN THE HIGHLIGHTED LETTERS AND UNSCRAMBLE THEM!

THE MYSTERY MOB IS...

THE NUMBERS SHOW THE NUMBER OF LETTERS IN EACH WORD!

ACROSS

5 You will need these if you want to glide through the air. (6)
6 If you want fish for your teatime, you're going to need one of these. (7,3)
9 If you break cobwebs with a sword, this is what you get. (6)
10 This is dropped by llamas, cows, horses and mooshrooms when they die. (7)
11 This is the mode you need if you want to build without worrying about being attacked. (8)
12 The company that brought Minecraft to life. (6)
13 The name of the adventure game created by Telltale Games. (5,4)

DOWN

1 This is what we call it when we combine blocks and items to make something new. (8)
2 It's a place filled with lava, fire and very dangerous mobs! (3,6)
3 If you put a Potato into a furnace with some fuel, this is what you will get. (5,6)
4 What grows on the back of Mooshroom mobs? (8)
5 You will need one of these if you want to go to The End. (3,6)
7 You can create incredible machines, or simple automatic doors, with these blocks to carry the power. (8)
8 He was the very first boss mob to be created in Minecraft and lives at The End. (5,6)
10 A large mob that lives in herds and spits. (5)

53

A MINECRAFT STORY

STRANGE THINGS can happen in the world of Minecraft. Come with us on a journey into another dimension as we bring you a tale of parties, digging and weird new friends... it's Minecraft story time!

"You should come," they said. "It'll be fun," they said. So, there I was that night - everything around me was as dark as a cave after the sun has gone to sleep. I felt like I'd stepped into a freezer, it was so cold. Nevertheless, I plodded over to my friend's house. Music boomed from inside and the raucous laughter of my friends rang throughout the world. Were they having a party? It's much worse: A birthday party!

Imagine turning up to a birthday party with no present?! Who even does that? Well, I was just about to, hence why I was in a bit of a pickle. Should I go in empty-handed and disappoint the birthday boy-or-girl? No, I couldn't bring myself to do that. Okay. "Think," I muttered to myself. I checked my pockets but all I had was a Fire Charge. Not the best birthday gift. Maybe I could find a present somewhere... somewhere else?

As all the shops were closed, and seeing no other alternative to finding a present, I decided to do the unthinkable and dig straight down - something I've been told you should never, ever do. I kept digging and digging in the hope of... maybe finding a Diamond? While I didn't find any shiny blues, I did accidentally stumble into another reality where I met these two... err... things. I think they said their names were "Tim" and "Drake".

"Jim" and "Snake", or whatever their names were, told me their world had been taken over by a dark evil so evil, it was eviler than the evilest evil at an evil convention of evil. It's pretty evil, I think was their point. I asked if they had any cake I could give as a late-to-the-party present, and they told me cake no longer exists in their world. What madness! This cannot be allowed to stand! No cake? NO CAKE?!

And so "Slim", "Steak", and myself journeyed to the far-reaches of their kingdom (or is that queendom?). We beat all manner of beasts, which is funny because you can't spell "Beasts" without "Beat", and eventually found our way into the Mice Bling's realm, or at least I think that was his name. Before us stood a tall ice structure. We knew that if we brought it down the world would revert back to its former beauty. But how would we beat a tower of ice?

We all looked at each other with puzzled faces. We were tired from our beast-beating. Plus I needed to get back to the

Loud music, lights... it could only be a birthday party!

One man and his dog... at least I think it was a dog!

It was scary in the other dimension!

party! "Kim" rummaged through his pockets, but came out empty-handed. "Quake" of course, didn't have any pockets on account of him being a dog. Then I had an even better idea than digging straight down. I went through my pockets and pulled out my Fire Charge. All our eyes gleamed as the three of us sent it hurtling towards the structure, only to watch it melt into a lake of stone cold water.

And with that, the world was back to the way it should be - bright colours plastered onto lovely landscapes. I said goodbye to my new friends, but not before they gave me the tastiest cake in all the lands, and I set off for home. I climbed back up my tunnel, cake in hand, and arrived back at the house. Everyone was still there, thankfully, so I ran as fast as I could to the door. So fast, I tripped on a rock and dropped the cake all over the floor... "WHHHYYY?" I cried.

After all of that I still didn't have a present. A crushing weight fell on my heart. I was going to be the guy who turns up to a birthday party with nothing. Oh the shame. The shame of it all! I stood, dusted myself off, and reached out to turn the doorknob. But before I could, the door swung open at a lightning speed. "Surprise!" they all shouted. "Come on in, we've got cake and presents." I pulled out my phone to check the date: October 31st. That's Halloween to you, but to me - my birthday!

You can't have a party without cake!

Make it!
CREEPER POPS!

HAVE A POP AT MAKING ME AS A CAKE POP!

INFO

CREEPER POPS!

TIME NEEDED: 60 MINUTES
EXTRA INFO: YOU NEED TO HEAT THE COLOURING OR IT WILL SPOIL YOUR CHOCOLATE!

YOU'LL NEED...

INGREDIENTS: 144g Rice Crispies Marshmallow Squares, 400g white chocolate, green food colouring, cake pop or kebab sticks, black icing pen, large grapefruit, tin foil.

DIFFICULTY

EASY
THESE ARE DEAD EASY TO MAKE AND LOOK GREAT AT PARTIES!

1 YOU BLOCKHEAD!

THE FIRST task is chopping up the Rice Crispies Squares into Creeper head-sized pieces. Ask an adult for help here. They won't make perfect cubes, but cut them in half to give nice sized chunks with a good face side for decorating. We're going to make 16 Creeper Pops out of 2 144g packets of Squares, then use 2, 400g bars of white chocolate for the coating. You can of course make more or less Creeper Pops if you wish, just change the quantities as you go! When you have your 16 blocks, push a stick into the centre of one of the smaller faces. Next, cover the grapefruit with tin foil and place it to one side – you will stick your Creeper Pops into this to set later.

CHOPPING A RICE CRISPIES SQUARE IN HALF GIVES A GOOD CREEPER HEAD-SIZED FACE!

2 I'M MELTING!

COMBINING WHITE chocolate with food colouring will need more adult help. First you need to warm the food colouring, so place the liquid bottle into a zip bag and heat it in warm water for 10 minutes. We do this as white chocolate can spoil if you add cold food colouring! Now melt the white chocolate in a bowl using the microwave, 30 seconds at a time. Give it a stir with a metal spoon between blasts, it should take about 90 seconds in total. Chocolate can easily burn, so be careful not to overheat. Once melted, add in the green food colouring a few drops at a time, mixing like crazy. Keep going until you have a nice Creeper shade of green!

3 PUT YOUR COAT ON

NOW TAKE each of your blocks on sticks and dip them in the green chocolate. Give them a spin to get fully coated, then stick them into your tin foil grapefruit. This will allow any drips to drip as they set. Continue with the other 15 Creeper Pops with a bit of speed, or the chocolate will set in the bowl! Now leave them to one side for 30 minutes, or pop them in a fridge if you can. Once set, use the black icing pen and draw a Creeper face onto each of the pops – there you go! Scary but sweet Minecraft Creeper Pops for your next party!

MAKE SURE YOUR GREEN CHOC BLOCKS SET HARD BEFORE YOU ICE ON THE CREEPER FACE!

PUZZLES
Test your brains with these teasers...

I BET YOU CAN'T FIND ME!

ANSWERS ON PAGE 93

MOB MAYHEM SEARCH!

INSIDE THIS giant letter grid are **12** **Minecraft Mobs**! First see if you can name them all – we've given you their faces and some letters to help. Then find them all in the wordsearch!

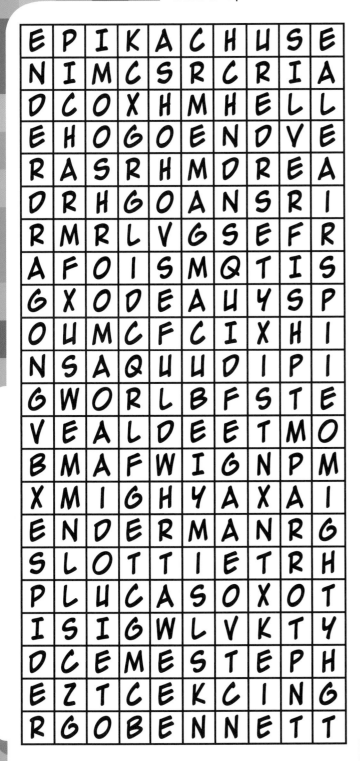

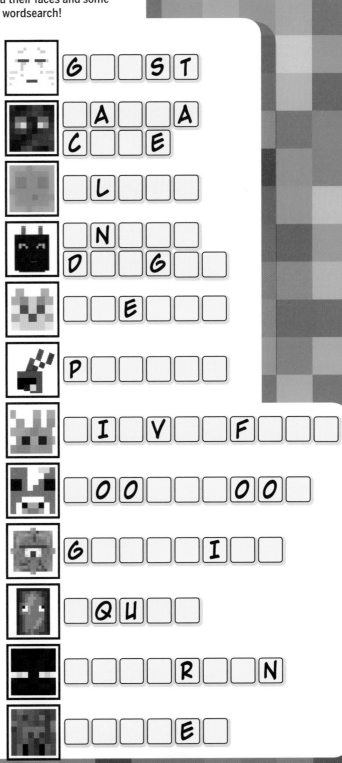

G _ _ S T

_ A _ _ _ A
C _ _ E _

_ L _ _ _

_ N _ _ _
D _ _ G _ _

_ _ E _ _

P _ _ _ _ _

_ I V _ _ F _ _ _

_ O O _ _ _ O O _

G _ _ _ _ _ I _

_ Q U _ _

_ _ _ _ _ R _ _ N

_ _ _ _ E _

20 MINUTES!

I MADE A RIGHT PIG'S EAR OF IT... FROM 3 PINK WOOL BLOCKS!

MINI MINECRAFT!

Tiny versions of our favourite characters for fun!

DIFFICULTY

NORMAL
THESE MINI MINECRAFT FIGURES CAN BE MADE BY ANYONE

MINI SLIME

You will need...
- Slime blocks
- Black Wool

1 TO KICK things off we're showing you how to turn a cube into a face. Getting this right means building every other mini Minecraft character should be a piece of cake. With your Slime blocks, build a 3x3, 3D cube. Knock out holes at the front for the eyes and add in Black Wool. Your Mini Slime lives!

MINI ENDERMAN

You will need...
- Black Wool
- Magenta Wool
- Green Hardened Clay
- Brown Hardened Clay

2 BUILD 3 blocks up for the legs of the Enderman, a 3x2 block for the body, 4 blocks out for each arm, and a 3x3 cube for the head. Add Magenta Wool for the eyes, then create a 2x3 Brown cube with a layer of Green Clay on top for the grass block.

MINI ZOMBIE

You will need...
- Black Wool
- Green Wool
- Cyan Wool
- Blue Wool
- Gray Wool

3 USE GRAY Wool (spellings in Minecraft are American) for the little Zombie's shoes then blue for the jeans. Build a 2x3 block for the T-shirt, add nubs on the side with the arms poking out, then a 3x3 cube for the undead head with Black eyes and that's your Mini Zombie complete.

MINI STEVE

You will need...
- Black Wool
- Brown Wool
- Cyan Wool
- Blue Wool
- Gray Wool
- White Wool
- White Hardened Clay

4 CREATE THIS one the same as the Mini Zombie, only this time make the legs 3-wide to accommodate Steve's massive head (which is a 4x5 block) and point the arms downwards. For the hair, replace the back of the head with Brown Clay and connect around to the front.

MINI CREEPER

You will need...
- Black Wool
- Green Wool

5 THIS ONE'S simpler than it looks. Drop down 4 blocks in a square formation with a 1-block gap between them. Build the body 4 high and 3 across, then finish up with a 3x3 box on top with the middle-left, middle-bottom and middle-right face blocks changed for Black ones.

You will need...
- Black Wool
- Green Wool
- Pink Wool
- White Wool
- Cobblestone
- Wood Fence

6 DESIGN THE same body shape as the Mini Zombie out of Pink Wool. Next, smash out the chest blocks and some of the face. In the gaps add White Wool for the skeletal parts and Green Wool for the slimy Zombie parts. Lastly, craft a Sword out of Cobblestone Walls and Fence for the handle.

MINI BLAZE

You will need...
- Black Wool
- Yellow Wool
- Brown Wool
- Yellow Hardened Clay

7 TO BRING a Mini Blaze to life create a 3x3 cube out of Yellow Wool. Replace the lowest layer with Brown Wool and add Black eyes to bring the face to life. For the fiery bits, just create random 3-high Yellow Wool pillars then replace 1 of the 3 blocks with Yellow Clay.

MINI SKELETON

You will need...
- Black Wool
- White Wool
- Light Gray Wool
- Spruce Wood Stairs

8 BUILD 2 blocks up in White Wool for the legs, but instead of building a chest, create a T-shape. Extend 1 arm out and 1 arm down and build the head with Light Grey Wool eyes. For the best Bow ever, put Stairs on either side of the hand section, then 1 more one block diagonally away on each side.

MINI WITCH

You will need...
- Black Wool
- Light Gray Wool
- Blue Hardened Clay
- Green Hardened Clay
- Orange Hardened Clay

7 DROP DOWN a row of 3 Light Gray Wool blocks for the feet, then build 3 up for the torso out of Blue and Green Hardened Clay. Extend the arms around the front of the body, create 1 last cube for the head, this time adding Orange Hardened Clay for the nose, and finish by building a hat out of Black Wool.

BUILD THESE!

MAYHEM ZOO

14 of the best Mo' Creatures mobs...

EVER WANTED to have your very own Minecraft zoo? Well our favourite game is so adaptable and customisable, and fans around the world are so clever in what they have made with Minecraft, that mods, resource packs and texture packs can make any dream come true!

We have been having lots of fun with the Mo' Creatures mod that was first created by DrZhark back in 2010, but is now up to version 6.3.1 for Minecraft 1.7.10. There are 79 new creatures in this mod, some of them are zoo favourites like lions, tigers, crocodiles and snakes. Others are more exotic like manta rays, komodo dragons and piranhas. Then there are the crazy creatures like a Wraith, Silver Skeleton or Ogre Prince!

On these pages we are showing off the 14 best creatures loved by our Minecraft experts, but first... to install Mo' Creatures in your Minecraft...

- Go to www.mocreatures.org/downloads

- Install **Forge** first. This is an add-on that allows you to install new mods into your game. The link downloads a .jar file, double click this to install.

- Now install the latest version of **Mo'Creatures** by clicking the link. Drop this .jar file into your 'mobs' folder then start a 'Forge' Minecraft game.

Grizzly Bear

WHILE YOU should never mess with a grizzly bear, this one is actually tamable! They naturally spawn on grass blocks, often with cubs alongside them (ahhhh). They will avoid cliffs and water, and wander around without doing very much. You can tame them when they are cubs by offering any basic Minecraft meat as a gift. You can even ride them!

Type: Tamable mob **Drops:** Hide
Spawns: Any solid surface with 2 blocks above

Top Tip: Watch out at night around bears – this is when they can get agressive and attack you. They will also attack other mobs, but not big cats – they're not stupid!

Lion

HE'S THE King of the Beasts and looks great in Minecraft graphics. Lions come in male and female versions, with the male having an impressive mane. When the world generates, Lions often appear in family groups of 4. There's a variety of big cats for different biomes, for example a Snow Leopard will spawn in snow biomes.

Type: Hostile mob **Drops:** Big Cat Claw
Spawns: Any solid surface with 2 blocks above

Top Tip: Many lions and other big cats will attack you on sight and have high speed, attack and health stats, so don't approach them without armoured protection.

WHAT DO YOU CALL A BEAR WITH NO 'EARS'? 'B'!

Elephant

NOBLE AND majestic, the elephant is an amazing animal. There are two types in Mo' Creatures – if it spawns in a snowy biome you get a Wooly Mammoth! You can tame and equip an elephant with a harness then travel around on it. They will only attack you if they are heavily provoked. You can hear them trumpeting in the distance.

Type: Neutral mob   **Drops:** Hide
Spawns: Opaque blocks at high light levels, often in herds of 3 at a time.

Top Tip: To tame one, you need to feed 10 sugar lumps or 5 cakes to an elephant calf. When it is fully grown you can dress it in garments.

Ostrich

YOU CAN find these flightless birds roaming around the Overworld in groups of 3 or 4. If you attack it, or one of its chicks, the ostrich will run around and stick its head in the ground. We don't recommend it though – the males are very agressive and they scream when killed!

Type: Neutral mob   **Drops:** Raw ostrich meat
Spawns: In flocks of up to 4

Top Tip: You can breed ostriches. First wait for a female to be alongside a male, then feed her a melon seed. In 2 minutes she will lay an egg.

DO I HAVE ANYBODY STUCK IN MY TEETH?!

Shark

WATCH OUT when swimming around the seas – sharks can grow from half a block wide to 1 block, and be up to 6 blocks long! They will come after you if you get within 16 blocks of them and can kill in 4 hits. Bizarrely they can be tamed by hatching a shark's egg in the water, you can then pull it out with a net.

Type: Hostile mob   **Drops:** Shark teeth
Spawns: In the sea if the water is at least 2 blocks deep and 8 blocks wide

Top Tip: If you must go into the water when a shark is around use a boat. Sharks won't attack a boat, but if you dangle your little legs in the water you will become their lunch!

EEK! SNAKES! WHY DID IT HAVE TO BE SNAKES?!

Snake

THERE ARE lots of different kinds of snake in Mo' Creatures, which one you get depends mainly on the biome they spawn in. Rattlesnakes are found in the desert, cobras in the jungle, green and orange snakes in the plains. While mainly passive, they are all capable of attacking you and have a nasty poison, so be careful!

Type: Hostile mob   **Drops:** Egg
Spawns: Any solid surface with 2 blocks above, and in the mysterious Wyvern Lair

Top Tip: Want to see a snake hunting? Drop a bird or mouse near the snake and it will spring into action – chasing the poor creature until it bites.

Turkey

GOBBLE GOBBLE! While the male turkeys have an impressive wattle (the red bit) under their necks and a fan of colourful feathers in the rear, the female turkeys are just plain old black and grey. They drop raw turkey meat when killed – now you can have a Christmas dinner! They really don't do much, just wander around making gobbling noises.

Type: Passive mob   **Drops:** Raw turkey meat and feathers   **Spawns:** On grass with 2 blocks above

Top Tip: Want a turkey to follow you into the amazing turkey trap you've built? Then you need to be holding melon seeds – they'll do anything for these!

I USED TO BE A WEREWOLF...

...BUT I'M ALRIGHT NOWWWWW!

Ant

OH YES, even the humble ant gets its own mob! They can climb up solid blocks and carry food items.

Werewolf

IT'S NOT all just zoo animals in Mo' Creatures – there are some weird and wonderful creatures in here too! They don't come much more weird than the werewolf. By day, it's a regular looking man, although his clothes are a bit tattered. By night – he turns into a howling werewolf! It's an amazing shape-shifter!

Type: Neutral mob   **Drops:** Golden apples, stone and iron items   **Spawns:** Any solid surface

Top Tip: There's only one weapon we would recommend for killing a werewolf – a silver sword! You can only get one of these from the silver skeletons, it can polish off a werewolf in only 4 hits.

Tiger

THESE STRIKING big cats have many similarities to the lions. They occasionally open their mouths to growl at passers by and swish their tails around when angry. They're not fussy what they chase for their dinner – anything from an ant, to a deer, to you will do! They are only aggressive when they are hungry though, they go quiet for a while once they have eaten.

Type: Hostile mob   **Drops:** Big Cat Claw
Spawns: Any solid surface with 2 blocks above

Top Tip: You can tame a tiger by using raw pork chops or raw fish when it is a tiger cub. You even get to name them – this one is called Tony.

Komodo Dragon

REACHING UP to 3 blocks long, the komodo dragon is as close to the fire breathing type you can get. They are a dangerous beast, and will chase you if you come within a 12-16 block radius of it, attempting to poison you! If you kill a komodo dragon and get its egg, you can create a tame one that you can ride.

Type: Venomous mob   **Drops:** Reptile hide
Spawns: Only in swampland biomes

Top Tip: The only known antidote to komodo dragon poison is Dirt Scorpion Armour. To make it you will need to craft with lots of Chitin, obtained from scorpions and manticores. (A manticore is a wierd lion/scorpion hybrid!)

Ogre

THERE ARE lots of different kinds of Ogre in Mo' Creatures. Some have one head, some have two heads, some are fire ogres that spawn in the Nether, others will spawn in small places and suffocate! During the day they are harmless, but at night they get quite angry and will chase you down.

Type: Neutral mob **Drops:** Obsidian blocks
Spawns: Anywhere that is big enough for one

Top Tip: Practise killing ogres by making sure you have good armour and preferably a diamond sword. You will need the practice as there's an Ogre Lair update coming to Mo' Creatures that will include an Ogre Prince boss!

I ALWAYS SAY THAT TWO HEADS ARE BETTER THAN ONE!

Kitty

WE'VE INCLUDED these adorable kitty cats just because we thought they were cute! Each time a kitty spawns, it has a different coat and colour, much like in real life! There are 8 variations in total. Just like real life cats, these start out wild but can be tamed, but they will still attack you if provoked! They will chase and kill anything smaller than themselves.

Type: Tamable mob **Drops:** Nothing
Spawns: Any solid surface with 2 blocks above

Top Tip: If you keep a kitty in your house, make sure you give it a litter box to do its business in. If you don't they can get angry and attack you. You can clean a used litter box with a sand block.

Ent

WHAT ON Earth is this creature? It's a giant walking tree called a Ent, and even has a tiny creature living in its trunk (can you spot the little red eyes?). The idea of the Ent is borrowed from the Lord of the Rings books by J.R.R. Tolkien. If you leave them alone they will create a 3x3 square of flowers, mushrooms, saplings, grass and ferns around them.

Type: Neutral mob **Drops:** Lots of wood **Spawns:** In groups of 4 on grass blocks with enough space above for their big heads

Top Tip: Ents are invulnerable to all forms of attack weapon, except for the axe. They have nightmares about axes! Beware though – if an Ent gets hold of you it will throw you high into the air!

MO' CREATURES isn't just all about the new mobs it introduces to Minecraft, there are also brand new blocks (like the Ogre Lair Leaves and Wyvern Lair Planks) and exciting items (like a Pet Amulet, Wyvern Portal Staff or Unicorn Horn). Alternate dimensions include the Wyvern Lair that is a spooky forest full of Wyvern creatures that you access by crafting a Wyvern Portal Staff, and in an upcoming update the Ogre Lair that is promised to be a scary floating island.

Just like in regular Minecraft you can choose to discover all of these new and exciting things as you play along in Survival Mode, or if you don't have the patience for that (or just want a house full of cute kitty cats) you can jump into Creative Mode and load up the Spawn Egg for the creature you want and spawn away! One thing is for sure – add-ons like Mo' Creatures are great fun to play around with and take your Minecraft game to a whole new dimension.

PLAYING MINECRAFT IN 3D!

Switch on 3D in your game, get yourself a pair of 3D glasses from a shop or the internet and let's play Minecraft in 3D...

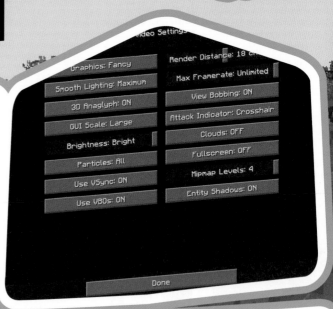

Video Settings

Graphics: Fancy	Render Distance: 18 c...
Smooth Lighting: Maximum	Max Framerate: Unlimited
3D Anaglyph: ON	View Bobbing: ON
GUI Scale: Large	Attack Indicator: Crosshair
Brightness: Bright	Clouds: OFF
Particles: All	Fullscreen: OFF
Use VSync: ON	Mipmap Levels: 4
Use VBOs: ON	Entity Shadows: ON

Done

SWITCH IT ON!

HAVE YOU ever seen that option, hidden away in the 'Video Settings' menu of Minecraft? 3D Anaglyph: OFF or ON! It makes the screen go very strange with lots of red and blue shadows all over it. Well there's a reason for that. An 'anaglyph' is a type of 3D photograph that has been around since 1853. That's 165 years to be precise! And your game of Minecraft has a hidden 3D option inside it!

3D GLASSES!

THESE SPECIAL 3D glasses often come free with magazines and comics, or you can find them in shops. Make sure you get the red and blue lense version, not the black ones you get at the cinema. If you can't find any in your local area, then ask your grown up to buy a pair from the internet for you. Places like ebay will have pairs of 3D glasses for just £1, and you can always use them as super-cool sunglasses if you want a unique look!

IT'S A TRICK!

FOR AS long as there has been photography, people have experimented with 3D pictures for one simple reason: our eyes are set slightly apart, and this is what makes what you see feel real. Close one eye and you will see what we mean. Your world will change to 2D and everything will feel flat. Open both eyes and you get a feeling of depth in everything around you. This is what 3D Anaglyph images try to trick your brain into seeing!

THE 3D GLASSES YOU GET IN MODERN MOVIES WON'T WORK, THESE USE A DIFFERENT SYSTEM OF 3D FILTERING, IT'S ONLY THE RED AND BLUE STYLE OF 3D THAT WORKS WITH MINECRAFT!

VISUAL SETTINGS

IN THE options of Minecraft click on the '3D Anaglyph' option in the 'Visual Settings' and select ON. Jump into the game in your favourite saved world and rather than seeing Minecraft in the usual 2D style, everything will have red and blue shadows all over it. The way it works is the bigger the shadows cast by objects, the closer or further away they seem to you in 3D! Let your eyes adjust to it.

THE WORLD IN 3D!

NOW TRY moving around, the clever boffins at Mojang created Minecraft with 3D Anaglyph visuals in mind, so every block, every object, every Mob – even the clouds – all change their 3D appearance depending on where you are standing in the world. The effect has often been tried in 2D and it was big for a while in movies, but to have a 3D game generating these 3D images in realtime is brilliant!

TRY THE 3D EFFECT IN MINECRAFT FOR JUST A FEW MINUTES AT FIRST AS IT GIVES SOME PEOPLE A HEADACHE. IF YOU'RE FINE, YOU CAN TRY AGAIN!

3 HOURS!

GLADIATOR COLOSSEUM!

The name means 'gigantic', and this is a BIG build. Create yourself a amphitheatre fit for Gladiators!

DIFFICULTY

HARD
THIS IS ONE GIGANTIC BUILD, A CHALLENGE TO KEEP YOU BUSY!

1

LAY THE FOUNDATIONS

GETTING THE circular foundation right is important to this build. To create this, grab some Stone then lay down the rows of blocks diagonally to one another in the following formation: 8,4,2,1,2,1,1 Turn to the right: 2,1,2, 4,8. To complete the circle, just keep repeating the formation until you have all 4 quarters connected.

2

BUILD IT UP

ONCE THE circular foundation is complete, build all the walls up by 3 blocks so they're all 4 high in total. Use this as an opportunity to see whether your groundwork is all level by standing in the middle and looking at the walls. If any don't match the walls opposite, then something has gone wrong. If all is OK, you're good to move on.

3

SAFETY FIRST

GRAB SOME Stone blocks and run them around the outside of the walls. Then with a Fence of your choosing, cover all the Stone blocks (this will act as your guardrail so no one falls into the pit). After that is complete, go around the outside of the Stone once more with yet another layer of Stone. It's taking shape!

4

TAKE YOUR TIME

NEXT, PULL some Stone Half Slabs from the Creative menu and lay them around the outside of the Stone blocks. Believe it or not, these Half Slabs are actually going to end up looking like seats in your Colosseum. It's also worth pointing out this next step is going to take you a while. It'll be worth it, though!

5

BUILD IT UP

NOW WE'RE going to repeat the last step again, only this time going around the Half Slabs one block out and up (like a step formation, almost). You'll need to do this a total of 12 more times to build up the sides of the amphitheatre. What you should be left with is a kind of bowl shape, which will act as the inside of your arena.

6

CONNECTING COLUMNS

PULL OUT your Stone bricks again and from behind the final row of Half Slabs, build a column going down. Now we're going to need to turn this column into a wall surrounding the outside of the arena, so let's build more columns parallel to the outer Half Slabs. You should end up with a solid Stone structure when viewed from the outside.

7

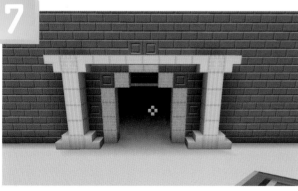

ROMAN PILLARS

PICK A wall and find its centre. Smash a 6x6 hole and create a door frame out of Chiselled Quartz Blocks. To the left and right, lay down Quartz Stairs, build a 5-high column out of Pillar Quartz then add Chiselled Quartz on top. On the other sides lay more Stairs, and also on both sides at the top. Connect the Quartz Stairs and you've got two Roman pillars.

8

A STAIRWAY UP

FROM THE centre of the door frame count 7 blocks in. With Stone bricks, build a stairway going up until you hit the half slabs. Now smash those half slabs out of the way. Use Stone to create a little platform at the end which should connect to flat half slabs (behind the Stone bricks and Stone block with fences on).

9

A BIG ENTRANCE

ON THE left and right sides of the stairs drop down some Quartz pillars. Build them up so they're 3 blocks higher than the front half slabs. Create a roof over the top and your entrance way into the arena, for the crowd, is complete. And don't forget to keep these last few steps in mind. You'll need them again later...

10

BUILDING A WALL

BACK AT the base of the stairs, 1 block diagonally away, build an 8-wide wall on both sides. To get some light in here, replace the middle 4 blocks with a light source of your choosing (we used Sea Lanterns). Underneath the light replace the Stone bricks with 2 Stone blocks and 2 Chiselled Stone blocks. Mirror this above the light source.

11

REPEAT ON OTHER SIDE

NEXT UP We're going to repeat steps 7 through to 10, but on the direct opposite side of your Colosseum. So that's: find the centre of the wall, smash it, build pillars, stairs, light source walls either side, add an entrance way. Try to get a feel for how pillars are built, too, as there's more pillar-building mayhem to come.

12

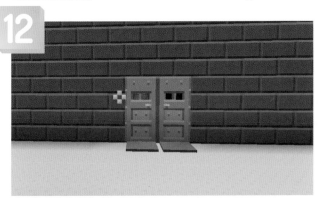

IRON DOORS

YOU SHOULD now be left with 2 outer walls in your gigantic building with nothing on them. Pick a wall, and in the centre punch a 4x2 hole and fill it with Iron Doors. Grab some Stone Pressure Plates and lay them in front of and behind the doors so they open easily and so no one gets locked in.

13

PREPARE FOR BATTLE

ON THE other side of the door, build a small room out of Stone bricks, and add in another door at the opposite end of the room leading into the arena area. And, of course, drop down some Pressure Plates once more so the door opens from either side. If you're going to use the arena for PvP battles, feel free to add in Chests full of loot now.

14

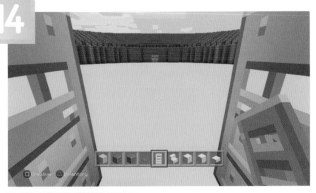

ONE MORE TIME

RUN STRAIGHT across the arena, smash in a door hole and fill it with Iron Doors. Just like we did before, add Pressure Plates, build a small room, add Chests if need be, and add a Door to the back wall for entry from the outside. Once all that's done your Gladiator Colosseum should be starting to take shape.

15

CONNECTING UP

HEAD BACK to the outside of the arena and look for your Quartz pillars. Level with where you joined up the Stairs at the top of the pillars, continue that row of Quartz half slabs all the way around the outside so it eventually connects back on itself. Don't worry about the solid Stone look of the outside, we'll be fixing that up later on.

16

FILL IN THE WALLS

BACK ON the inside, by the stairs, we're now going to fill in the walls. On the left and right of the light source walls, build a column that's 1 block out. Add another next to it, then another light source wall just like the one you've already built. Curve it around to the wall behind you, build it again where needed, and you're done here.

17

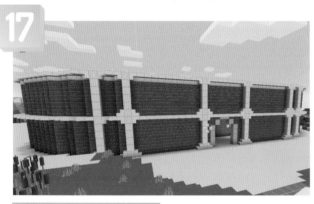

BUILDING PILLARS

NOW WE'RE fixing up the outside. Add in a row of Chiselled Stone around the top followed by a row of Quartz blocks on top of that. Add pillars on the far left and right sides of the main wall, and more pillars on the smaller walls. Next, continue the pillars upwards so they're level with the Quartz blocks.

18

A STRONG STRUCTURE

AFTER YOU'VE run Quartz slabs all around the top of the upper pillars, head to the sides with the Iron Doors. Build pillars to the left and right of the doors, more pillars a few blocks away from those, and again on the smaller walls. With these last 2 steps, don't forget to build them again on the opposite sides.

19

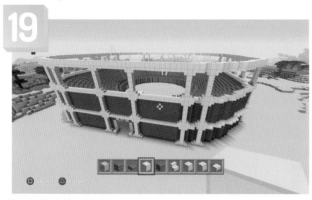

BIG IS BEST!

IT'S TIME to build our upper area of the Gladiator arena. On every pillar build another one sitting on top of it. Don't worry, it will take the weight! After all your pillars are built, connect the tops, from step-to-step, with Quartz half slabs. Now, above the half slabs add Quartz blocks so they run all around the top.

20

IMPRESSIVE WALLS

BACK INSIDE the arena, go to the Iron Doors. Move up past the Fence and 1 block away from the Stone rim, lay down 2 Stone bricks with a 2 block gap. Behind them add a column of bricks/stone/bricks and connect it up. Build a wall behind it with pillars at each end. Add in a Quartz stripe horizontally as well as the window area.

21

BUILD A SKYBOX

BEHIND THE pillars, build the walls out by 5 blocks then end on another Stone pillar. Create the roof by adding a platform of Quartz blocks surrounded by half slabs. For the insides, a seat can be made out of 2 Wooden blocks with turning corners. Add armour stands on a platform with heads on top to make it look like there are people inside.

22

TWO BY TWO

WITH ONE skybox complete, it's time to head on over to the opposite side and build another. After all, symmetry really does help to bring this arena to life. Build it just like in the last step. Chiselled bricks to start, then pillars, then walls, then the roof, then the inside. Use this also as a chance to zoom out and admire your handiwork.

23

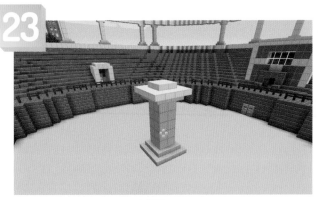

A CENTRAL PILLAR

RUN BLOCKS coming from the centre of each entry way to determine the middle of the arena and lay down a 4 square of Pillar Quartz (then break away the other blocks). Build the pillars up so they're all 7 blocks tall. Run Stairs around the bottom, then upside-down Stairs around the top, and finish by placing half slabs in the middle.

24

DECORATIVE QUARTZ

BACK ON the outside, where the Quartz blocks sit on the pillars, add 2 more rows of Quartz all the way around. To create this lovely pattern effect in the solid Quartz, all you need to do is smash a 3x3 hole directly above the pillars then place Stairs in the corners of the hole before dropping a block in the top-middle with Stairs attached either side.

25

OPTIONAL EXTRA

THIS PATHWAY is entirely optional. If you prefer the sandy look of the floor inside, feel free to stick with that. If not, dig a trench from each of the doors to the pillar in the middle and lay down Cobblestone. You could also add 2 more doors on the empty walls if you want to turn this into a 4-player PvP battle map! Well done, an impressive build!

PUZZLES

Test your brains with these teasers...

HOW GOOD DO YOU THINK MINECRAFT IS?

HIDDEN ITEMS CRISS-CROSS

WE'VE STUFFED this criss-cross puzzle with **Minecraft items**. Could be **raw materials, manufactured items, food, plants** – you'll have to answer the clues and slot in the words, testing your Minecraft knowledge. Then take the letters from the **yellow highlighted squares** and unscramble them to find the **mystery item**! You will find all the answers on page 93.

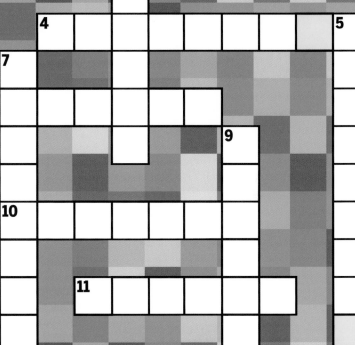

I THINK IT'S TOP NOTCH!

ANSWERS ON PAGE 93

THE MYSTERY ITEM IS...

THE NUMBERS SHOW THE NUMBER OF LETTERS IN EACH WORD!

ACROSS

1 The main use of this item is to get Wool from Sheep. (6)

4 You can protect your feet with this armour by crafting with Iron Ingots. (4,5)

8 This is a raw fish, but is highly poisonous to eat. (10)

10 These green items are used as money for Villager trading. (7)

11 This protection item can be crafted from Wood Planks and Iron Ingot. (6)

12 This item shows the sun and moon's position. (5)

DOWN

2 If you want to locate and activate End Portals you will need to craft one of these with Blaze Powder and Ender Pearl. (3,2,5)

3 You can make one of these from Wheat and Cocoa Beans, but you shouldn't eat too many! (6)

5 These small round items are dropped by Slimes when they are killed. (9)

6 These aren't for Easter, they're for creating animals. (5,3)

7 Smelt some Netherrack in a Furnace with fuel and you will get one of these. (6,5)

9 You can put one of these on some mobs to go for a ride! (6)

DETECTOR RAIL ROLLER COASTER

Building with Red Stone...

90 MINUTES!

START HERE!

1 ROLLER COASTERS are great fun to build in Minecraft, and we're going to show you how to take them to the next level with Detector Rails. First, plan out the layout of your coaster with Wood blocks, have areas that are flat and areas that go up and down to give the riders a thrill!

2 TO ATTRACT thrill seekers your roller coaster has got to be attractive. Add in things like a flag, Vines creeping up over the wooden structures, Cactuses and lakes. We want to give the impression there are mysteries to be uncovered as you ride to make people want to queue!

3 USING NORMAL Rails, lay out the roller coaster track on top of the wooden blocks all the way around your coaster. This will be the basic track that you can add to with more complicated rails and features later. Sadly, you can't ride it yet as we've not placed any Powered Rails.

4 YOUR COASTER is going nowhere until these Powered Rails are added. Add them on every steep bit, after each corner or wherever you want to give the riders a boost. The Powered Rails need power – either place hidden Redstone Torches under the track, or a Lever next to the track and switch it on.

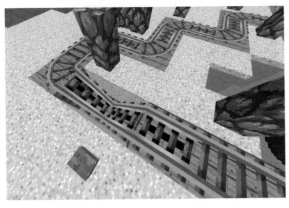

5 THIS IS the start and end of the coaster. Create a section of Powered Rail with a dip to stop the Minecart so that the riders can get on and off. Place a Button next to the Powered Rail which will act as a starter to get the Minecart going. Buttons power the rail only for a short time, unlike Levers.

6 HERE COME the Detector Rails! By placing a Detector Rail on the track and Dispensers either side of the track you can have the Minecart trigger an event to make the coaster more exciting! Dispensers are great – they will 'dispense' whatever you put inside. We put Fireworks in ours!

7 THE GRAND finale of our roller coaster is a shocking encounter with a spitting Llama! What we want is the Minecart to pause in front of him so riders risk being spat at. So we added a Detector Rail to set off Redstone under the coaster with Repeaters set to 4 Ticks. Play with your timings to get it right.

8 NEXT TO the Llama we have built a dip in the track out of Powered Rails, this is the track that the Redstone and Repeaters are going to power. So the riders get stuck with a Llama staring and spitting at them, just as they think it's going to come at them the track is powered again and off they go!

9 NOW THAT you know all the secrets of Powered Rails and Detector Rails you can build roller coasters of any size and type! We continued to expand ours with a second crazy Llama wearing a blue carpet and the vines grew all over our Wooden blocks. Don't forget the golden rule – always exit through the gift shop!

BUILD THIS!

I WOULDN'T SAY I'M CRAZY. I JUST LIKE A BOOGIE NOW AND AGAIN

KNOW YOUR MINECRAFT BLOCKS!

The secret to success in Minecraft is knowing which block does what! Here's everything you need to know about the block *Obsidian!*

MY DIAMOND PICKAXE IS THE ONLY THING THAT WILL CUT THROUGH OBSIDIAN!

 1 Obsidian forms when a flowing water source meets a fiery Lava plume.

 2 It takes exactly 9.375 seconds to mine a block of Obsidian with a Diamond Pickaxe.

 3 Mining Obsidian with a diamond pickaxe while underwater would take you 3 mins 54 secs.

 4 Obsidian cannot be blown up by Creepers, making it a great block to fortify houses with.

 5 In the real world, Obsidian is a natural glass that's formed by the rapid cooling of lava.

 6 In the original tests of Minecraft, Obsidian would only drop one or two pieces of Cobblestone.

 7 The minimum size of a Nether Portal is 4x5 Obsidian blocks, while the maximum is a whopping 23x23!

 8 Even though Obsidian is Creeper-proof, it's not safe from The Wither's blue skull projectile.

 9 It would take around 71.25 times the power of TNT to blow up one block of Obsidian.

 10 Non-boss mobs can travel through Obsidian Nether Portals. So be sure to look behind you when entering or leaving!

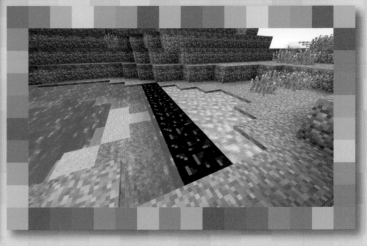

PUZZLES
Test your brains with these teasers...

HAVE YOU GOT BRAINS? I'M REALLY HUNGRY!

WEAPON SUDOKU

CAN YOU fill in the blank squares with weapons, making sure that each row of 4 has only one of each? Oh, and each block of 4 also has to have only one of each. Draw in the missing weapons and we'll see how much of a brain box you are!

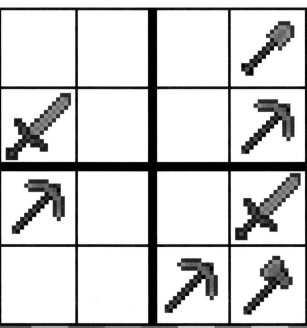

NAME THAT BLOCK

WHAT WOULD a game of Minecraft be without blocks? They come in all shapes, sizes, colours (and smells?). How well do you think you know your Iron Ore from your Coal? Now is the time to shine...

ANSWERS ON PAGE 93

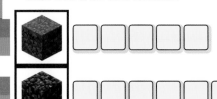

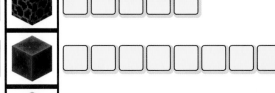

HAVE YOU GOT THEM ALL RIGHT? THE ANSWERS ARE ON PAGE 93

HOW MANY SPIDERS?

WOAH LOOK OUT! Our world has been overrun by deadly spiders. Maybe it's our deodorant attracting them? While we find a sword to sort them out, can you count how many there are? Can you spot the bonus rabbit?

WRITE IN HOW MANY YOU FOUND!

MORNING MUM!

JUST LIKE a Pokémon game on Nintendo 3DS you start out in your house, only this time you are in Serenity Town, with your mum downstairs making breakfast! You can chat with her, and other characters you meet, to find out more about what's going on in Suliqu region. Keep talking with mum and she will give you a Soda Pop and some dollars to spend. "Thanks mum!"

ITEM SEARCHING

EXPLORE AROUND the town to get used to your surroundings. You can find items like Burn Heal and Potions in Poké Balls that are worth picking up and storing for later. You won't be able to leave the town though until you have visited the theatre, found Professor Cedar, chatted with her daughter then found the Prof's lab.

INFO

POKÉMON COBALT & AMETHYST

TIME NEEDED: 60+ HOURS
EXTRA INFO: WORKS IN VANILLA MINECRAFT, SO NO NEED TO INSTALL ANY MODS

WOW! MINECRAFT MEETS POKEMON – THE ULTIMATE MASH-UP!

POKÉMON COBALT & AMETHYST

Getting started in the new Pokémon adventure!

YOU WILL never believe it! Some clever game designers calling themselves Phoenix Projects have gone and created a mash-up of Minecraft and Pokémon! While this is not an official Pokémon game, it's very professional, and packed with Pokémon fun to discover! Let's take Pokémon: Cobalt & Amethyst for a spin...

DIFFICULTY

★★★

HARD
THERE'S POKÉMON BATTLING TO DO, YOU WILL NEED TACTICS!

MEET THE PROF

PROFESSOR CEDAR and her daughter Kaylene can be found in town. Chat with them before heading to the store for a Rare Candy. After further chats with Kaylene back at her house, you will end up in the lab with the Prof. She will have a package for you to deliver to Timicin near the exit to Route 16. He'll be so pleased he will give you a Waiver that will give access to Route 17 and get you out of the town!

A MAP OF THE MAP

TO GET around the various areas of the Suliqu region you're going to need a map! Luckily your mum should have shown you one back at home, so just Right Click to bring it up whenever you need it. The Cobalt & Amethyst creators tell us there are 60-80 hours of gameplay to be enjoyed here, with puzzles for all abilities and of course the all-important Pokémon battling! All the 130 Pokémon are brand new ones, made up for the game.

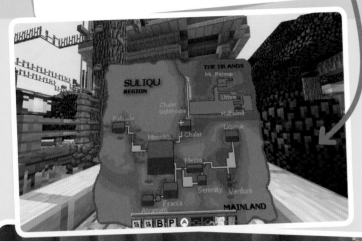

HOW TO GET IT...

POKÉMON
Cobalt & Amethyst

A 1.8.8 VANILLA MINECRAFT MAP

Phoenix SC, Phoenix Projects 2017

YOU CAN download this Pokémon map by following the link on the YouTube video of the game (ask whoever looks after you for permission first). Just search "Pokemon Cobalt and Amethyst" to find it. To play the map you will need to set your Minecraft game to run in version 1.8.8. You do this from the Launch Options menu before you start the game.

TEAM TEMPEST

EXCITING! Follow Professor Cedar down Route 17 and you will meet two Team Tempest grunts called Jason and Melissa who are blocking your way. The Prof will give you your first Pokémon – a Pyraiz Fire type Pokémon at Level 5! Little Pyraiz will evolve into a new Pokémon when it reaches level 30. Melissa will take you on in your first Pokémon battle using her level 5 Joulebo Pokémon.

FIRST BATTLE

THE SCREEN will go all wavy and you will be transported to a Pokémon battle arena with a Poké Ball symbol on the ground. This early in the game you will need to experiment with the moves you have available to see which will work best against the Pokémon you're up against. There's no time to stop to see how cute these Pokémon are! This won't be a very tricky battle, you can use a Potion if you really need to, and your little Pyraiz will level up and learn the new move Ember! With Melissa beaten, Jason will take you on.

PICK A POKÉMON!

WITH THE Team Tempest Grunts beaten, and a quick friendly battle with Cedar completed, head on back to the Professor's Lab and she will invite you to pick your first proper Pokémon. There are three on offer: Elerind, a Grass type that looks like a cute green bunny, Laviem is a Fire Pokémon and looks like a small black block and Krillbard, a Water Pokémon, looks a bit like a Silverfish from Minecraft! Which one will you choose?

MESSO TOWN

ON WITH your journey! The other side of Route 17 you will find Messo Town. It's a very rocky place so explore to get your bearings. You will need to find Kaylene, Professor Cedar's daughter, she's near the entrance to a cavern. She's a naughty girl and doesn't want her mum to know she's this far away from home, she'll offer to battle you if you keep quiet! To defeat her you really need to have your Pokémon on at least level 10, so do some battling to level up – good luck!

POKÉMON CENTRE

IT'S ALWAYS worth stopping off at the Pokémon Centres you come across in your adventure. Nurse Joy is inside and will ask if you want your Pokémon restoring to full health – always worthwhile in case you get jumped on by wild Pokémon in the long grass! There are extra Poké Balls and TM moves dotted around the map too, so look out for those. We found the Ground type move Dig that can come in handy if you want to escape from a battle quickly!

CONTINUE YOUR ADVENTURE

AND THAT'S just for starters! By the time you reach the end of this tutorial stage in Cobalt & Amethyst you will know how to control the game, how to battle Pokémon and who the main characters are. There is so much to see and do, but a word of warning. Whenever a chat window opens up you need to step your way through the chat carefully. If you escape out of it you can break the game and have to start over. The game designers recommend you regularly back up your game world folder so that you can always reload and try again.

HOW DO YOU GET 10 PIKACHUS IN A CAR? YOU POKE-'EM-ON!

PIXELMON
...and there's more Pokémon fun!

1 SINCE 2012

PIXELMON IS another fan made mod for Minecraft, completely unofficial and nothing to do with Pokémon or Nintendo. The fans have lovingly recreating many of the gameplay elements of Pokémon in Minecraft though, including Pokémon Battling, and it's great fun to play. Find out how to download and get the game running for you at pixelmonmod.com

2 GYMS

JUST LIKE the regular Pokémon games, there are Gyms with Gym Leaders inside for you to challenge. We met Greg from the Ivy Gym – nice man. He had a whole set of mazes in the long grass, with Trainers who will battle you each step of the way. There are badges for beating the Gym Leader at the end of the Gym.

4 TRADING

SO YOU'VE got some Pokémon, but they're the ugly ones that no-one likes. What do you do? Trade! You can find traders all over the map and they will be looking for a particular type of Pokémon, and will give you a specific one in exchange. This is a great way of getting the cooler Pokémon like little Pikachu, the electric mouse, himself!

5 BATTLING

IF YOU see a Pokémon that you would like to battle you just throw your best Pokémon at it (press R) in its Poké Ball. You will level up your Pokémon with each victory, and that's the secret to doing well in any Pokémon game! Gotta fight 'em all!

3 PACKED WITH POKÉMON

WHILE THIS game is full of Pokémon goodness, you will also still have to do all the usual Minecraft Survival things like find food, cook it and make yourself a shelter. Only now you will have a bunch of Pokémon to stay the night with you! Be sure to get in touch and tell us which Pokémon you find.

A MUSHROOM KINGDOM!

No, it's not Mario's kingdom, but it's pretty close!

CREATING YOUR very own colourful fairyland to play about in requires plenty of unique imagination, but here are a few ideas from us on how to craft your very own toadstool and mushroom-festooned magical place!

THERE'S NOT MUSH-ROOM WITH ALL THESE TOADSTOOLS ABOUT!

1

NUKE IT!

▶ **WE NEED** to find a nice flat area and then nuke it with TNT! What you'll want to end up with is a 17x17 square hole that's around 7 blocks deep. You'll be using TNT to do most of the work, don't worry about it being perfect, clear up later.

2

FUNGAL GROWTH

▶ **NEXT PULL** out the White Mushroom Block and find the rough middle of the hole. Now go ahead and create a 6x6 square. Now you're good to build the walls up high enough so they tower over the rest of the world – but don't hit the clouds.

3

BASE TOWER

▶ **NOW ADD** shaping to the rectangle, which we'll call the Base Tower. Using Mushroom, draw diagonal lines in any formation heading up each of the sides. Build up from the ground to meet the lines. With 4 done, add random shapes to decorate.

4

UNDER MY ROOF

▶ **COUNT 7** blocks down from the top. Work out where the middle of each side is, mark the middle 2 blocks with Mushrooms. Now build each 17 blocks from the Base Tower. From the end of the arms, build and join the 4-long sections of what will be our red dome.

5

THE DOME

▶ **BUILD UP** each of the 4 4-wide arms so they stand 6 blocks tall. Then add 5 blocks behind, then 4, 3, 2, and 2 sets of 1. You should now be able to connect the 4 sections across the top. Now just build up the other sections the same way.

6

LOOK UNDERNEATH

▶ **ON THE** underside of the giant mushroom, build a 1-high rim on the inside, then a 2-high rim behind that, and fill in the ceiling. Go back to the red top and smash out sections at random and then replace with White Wool.

7

LIGHT UP TIME

WITH THE top finished, your stem will now be bathed in darkness. To fix this, just grab Ender Rods and run them from the ceiling and along the stem, then place a Sea Lantern at the bottom. Now you'll be able to see what's what!

8

WIN THE POOLS

CHECK TO make sure the distance from stem to wall are all the same, then use Polished Diorite to create the pool. Add Sea Lanterns, then fill up. Now go around and find the centre of each of the 4 walls and knock out a few blocks to mark them.

9

FILL HER UP

USE DIRT blocks to make the floor level with the pool area. Run Dark Oak Fence around outside. Now go back to the middle of each wall, and create 4 sets of 5-wide Steps leading all the way back up to ground-level, and add Torches.

10

LEAFY STUFF

GRAB A Leaf Block and create 4 3-wide, 3-high hedges on both sides of all steps. Now connect them in a diagonal fashion. With Polished Diorite, create the step/leaf combo 1 block higher than the steps on the left and right of the main steps.

11

GARDENING TODAY

FROM BEHIND the Diorite lay down Grass Blocks. Then 1 block up and behind, more! Repeat until you have 4 rows, including the row level with the Diorite. Run Diorite up the sides and connect round the back-top. Add Flowers to your heart's content!

12

FIRST HOUSE

MAKE A 11x7 rectangle. At the back, lay down a 5x5 square for the rear. Build all corners up by 4 blocks, add in a doorway, then front wall and connect White Mushroom along the top. Fill walls with Dirt, then add front and back roofs.

THE  KINGDOM

13

HOLY SHROOMS!

DO MUSHROOM people have churches? Well they do now! Start with the Door Frame, add 2 rows above, then place in the poking out bits on the sides. Now mirror the bottom, only above. Lay down the mushrooms on top in a step formation...

14

CHURCH HALL

BELOW THIS Mushroom staircase, you should be able to create walls leading downward. Create the back section while taking note of the shape of the structure, and fill in the windows and add a mini-roof at the back. Your fungi church is done!

15

BLACKSMITH FORGE

START WITH your 3 Quartz steps then place blocks behind either side with Fence on. Build Fence up by 3, then place blocks on top. Build along so the front is 10 blocks long. Add in the room on the left, and the forge area on the right.

LEGO HAS already beaten you to it! LEGO set 21129 is a Minecraft Mushroom Island, complete with red and white giant mushroom and Mooshroom roaming around causing trouble.

WHILE IT'S easy to build these LEGO Minecraft sets, the fun is in playing with the characters and locations once you've built it.

YOU'VE GOTTA love the LEGO Minecraft Creepers and Mooshroom! LEGO don't often make new pieces, preferring to use the millions they have already made, but these Creeper legs are unique!

16

ACACIA AVENUE

CAN YOU see how all the trees look out of place? Don't worry, we're going to rebuild them out of our 2 Mushroom blocks. Acacia Trees work the best here due to their natural shape, but any tree will do. Experiment with what you have to hand!

17

MUSHROOM FOR ALL!

NOW JUST hack away the leaves on top of the tree and replace with Red Mushroom, then chop down the wooden trunk section and change it to White Mushroom, and that's this build completed! Invite all your friends around for a Quorn feast!

THIS IS THE PLACE TO BE IF YOU'RE... A FUN GUY!

PUZZLES
Test your brains with these teasers...

IF YOU FIND ONE PROBLEM TOO HARD, TRY AN UDDER ONE!

TRACKBLOCK

THIS BLOCK hides three 9 letter words connected to our favourite videogame! Can you find them all?

T F A
I N R
O P M E G
T E B H E
L F E O S F
O O W K

ANSWERS ON PAGE 93

HIDDEN BLOCKS

THIS WORD BLOCK has the names of four different types of block frozen inside it – can you draw a line from letter to letter to find out which types are hiding in there?

SPOT THE DIFFERENCE

HOW MANY differences do you think there are between these two pictures from Minecraft: Story Mode? It's more tricky than you may think! Write your number below.

PICTURE 1

G M S M
E R E A
M L A G
I S O M
S M A N

PICTURE 2

WRITE IN HOW MANY YOU THINK!

DIFFICULTY

HARD
YOU NEED TO FOLLOW CLOSELY
TO GET YOUR SLIME WORKING

60 MINUTES!

THE SLIME BLOCK RAILWAY!

Forget Thomas... the future is Slime Block railways! Here's our step-by-step mega-build...

INFO

SLIME BLOCK RAILWAY

TIME NEEDED: 1 HOUR
EXTRA INFO: GOOD TRAINING IN HOW TO COMBINE SLIME, NETHER AND REDSTONE.

THERE'S SO much fun to be had in Minecraft building railways, minecarts, roller coasters and other cool machines. Have you tried combining the impressive might of Slime blocks, Nether bricks and Redstone though? In this mega-build we're going to show you how to build an impressive railway station and train first, then step-by-step how to fire up your engine with Slime blocks and watch it go! You can take the techniques you learn here and use them to create some impressive machines to show off to your friends. So...

STICK WITH ME AND I'LL SHOW YOU HOW TO MAKE A RAILWAY!

86

1

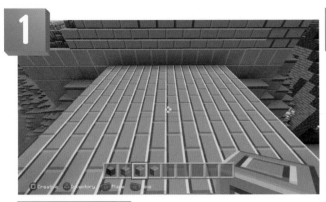

FIND A SPACE

LET'S BEGIN by finding a gigantic open space, preferably the side of a mountain with nothing opposite giving plenty of room for building. From here build a platform that's **7 blocks** out of the mountain and **8 blocks** across. Next, fill your hotbar with **Spruce** wood, **Stone** bricks, **Chiselled Stone** bricks and **Stone**.

2

MAKE A PLATFORM

BUILD 2 rows of **Chiselled Stone** bricks on the left and right side of the platform **33 blocks** in length. Then from the left count **1 block** and on the second block drop in a row of **Stone** also **33 blocks** long. Head over to the right side and do this again. Grab your **Spruce Wood** and place horizontal rows with a gap in-between each section.

3

COLUMNS

ONCE YOUR railway line is complete, head back to the start. On the right where the **Chiselled Stone** brick starts add 2 more **Chiselled Bricks** to the outside. On this **2x2** section build each corner up **11 high**. Back on the Chiselled row count **1 block** out and with a **Cobblestone** wall, place 10 of them on top of each other.

4

TIME FOR A BRIDGE

LET'S COUNT a block out and build a spike that's **9 high**. Miss a gap and build one **8 high**. Keep doing this until you get down to a **4 high** spike, then add another **4 high** spike **1 block** away from it. Repeat the process, only in reverse until you're back up to a second **10 high** **Cobblestone** wall. The walls should look symmetrical.

5

TOWER OF POWER

RIGHT OFF the last spike build a **2x2 tower 11 high**. For a bridge, grab **Stone Brick Slabs** and place them on top of all of your spikes, fill in the gaps with slabs half a block higher. They look like a row of steps. Delete the right side of the **Chiselled Brick** row at the bottom and replace it with **Stone Half-Slabs** so the railway line slightly pokes out.

6

DOWN TO GROUND

BACK AT the first **2x2 tower**, build it down to ground or water level. At the base of the tower cover the outside in a **4x4 square**. Now build another **4x4 square** on top of that. Next place **Stone Brick** steps going around the top of the square. Head to the top of the tower and add another **4 Stone Steps** at the top and this tower is complete.

7

COMPLETE THE BRIDGE

HEAD TO the other tower and repeat the step 6 instructions to finish it up. You'll also now need to create another two towers on the left Chiselled Stone Brick row opposite your already complete towers and add in some spikes and Half-Slabs. Once completed, your bridge should be looking fantabulous.

8

BUILD A STATION

WE FIRST need to build a brick shape as the foundation. Turn around and look at the end of the tracks. On the far-left side (coming off the tower) build with Bricks: 3 out, 4 left, 6 down, 4 left, 14 down, 4 right, 6 down, 4 right. Then on the right side we build it again but in reverse: 3 out, 4 right, 6 down, 4 right, 14 down, 4 left, 6 down, 4 left.

9

EXTEND THE TRACKS

ONCE THE shape is complete, extend your railway tracks so they meet the end of the shape. Then it's back to the Brick shape. Build all the walls 2 high. Now on every corner build a 3 high wall. To finish grab some Iron Bars and fill in the gaps between the corners you've just laid down leaving only the longest sides empty.

10

TICKETS PLEASE

ON EACH side of the tracks add Coal blocks so people don't stand too close to the tracks. Then fill in the floor area with Stone blocks. In the gaps we didn't fill in build a 4 high door frame out of Quartz blocks and Half Quartz Slabs. Around the left side of the doorway build a wall out of Bricks, Glass panes and Quartz Half-Slabs for a ticket booth.

11

LIGHTS, ACTION!

HEAD TO the outside of the booth and build walls, a floor and 4 more ticket booths on the inside. Then, add a carpet of your choosing on the floor. Build the walls 4 out then create a box shape to turn our ticket booths into a cube structure. Add Sea Lanterns into the ceiling to create some light. After all, no one likes working in the dark.

12

ROOF & STEPS

ADD QUARTZ Half-Slabs around the roof and you're done. Although, you may want to add steps if your booth is floating in mid-air. Head on back to the opposite door frame and add a 3 high Brick wall with Quartz Half-Slabs on the top to match the door frame. Again, add some steps on the other side of the door so people can actually reach the platform.

13

THE SLIME BLOCK TRAIN

EMPTY YOUR hotbar and fill it with Black Wool, a Slime block, a Redstone block, a Piston, a Sticky Piston, Nether Brick Fence and Nether Brick Stairs. At the start of the track place 2 blocks 1 block apart. On top of that place Black Wool then 3 Slime blocks above in a line. Delete the first 2 blocks you placed so the back of the train floats.

14

FUN WITH FUNNELS

ADD TWO more Slime on the left and right then 1 block behind each. Behind the middle Slime add a Piston facing it. On the other side of the middle Slime place a Sticky Piston facing the back of the train, then in front of that another Piston facing out. Drop a row of 3 Slime blocks coming off the Piston and a Nether Brick Fence on top of the last block to act as the funnel.

15

ALL ABOARD...

ADD ONE Slime block under the first and third of the new row you placed. On both sides of these blocks add Black Wool to look like wheels. Grab your Nether Brick Stairs and place 1 on the base of the front of the train. To power this awesome beast, drop a Redstone block on the back-half of the front and another one more at the back. Now all that's left to do is place a Redstone block to the left of the Sticky Piston, delete it, and your train should chug along your track. Great work!

INSPIRATION

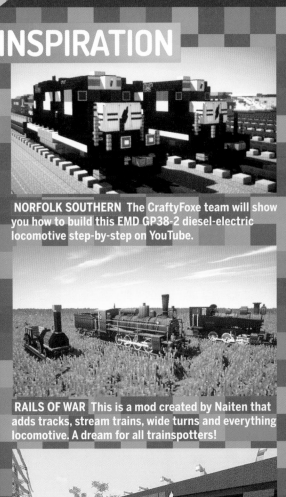

NORFOLK SOUTHERN The CraftyFoxe team will show you how to build this EMD GP38-2 diesel-electric locomotive step-by-step on YouTube.

RAILS OF WAR This is a mod created by Naiten that adds tracks, stream trains, wide turns and everything locomotive. A dream for all trainspotters!

TRAINS IN GREENFIELD The Minecraft Transp Co has an entire server dedicated to trains and railways of all kinds. Google it for more info!

PUZZLES

Test your brains with these teasers...

ROUND AND ROUND THE SECRET CODE GOES!

ROUND 'N' ROUND CODE

TAKE A close look at the circle of letters here. Somewhere hidden away in these letters is a secret phrase about an important part of Minecraft. One clue: you need to skip a letter each time to uncover the secret phrase. Another clue: Check out the picture in the middle. Can you find the secret message?

HOW MANY PARROTS?

THESE SQUAWKING birds get everywhere, tweeting and pooping all over the place. How many can you count in this picture? Hands up if you can spot the bonus Skeleton!

WRITE IN HOW MANY YOU THINK!

FIND THAT BLOCK CRISS-CROSS

THIS CRISS-CROSS crossword puzzle has 12 Minecraft block clues. See if you can fill in all the answers, then unscramble the letters highlighted in yellow to reveal a famous Minecraft Mob! We have also placed the blocks around the page to help you out!

CAN YOU FIND ALL THE MINECRAFT ANSWERS?

ANSWERS ON PAGE 93

THE MYSTERY MOB IS...

THE NUMBERS SHOW THE NUMBER OF LETTERS IN EACH WORD!

ACROSS

3 You must mine these blocks to get the stuff that powers Minecraft. (8,3)
6 You would look great wearing one of these at Halloween! (4,1,7)
7 Got a horse or llama to feed? You need some of these blocks. (3,4)
8 You can use this block to remove water from an area. (6)
9 These black blocks are incredibly strong and can only be mined with a Diamond Pickaxe. (8)
11 Found in the Nether, these blocks emit light and can burn. (5)
12 If you hit one of these blocks you had better stand well back! (3)

DOWN

1 If you want to hear some music, you will need one of these (7)
2 Coming in 16 colours, these blocks used to be known as Hardened Clay. (10)
4 This is a special block that can pull another block towards it. (6,6)
5 An indestructible block that sits underneath everything. (7)
10 If you smash this block with a shovel it turns into Snowballs. (4)

Activity
Make it!
PIG OPEN SANDWICH!

WARNING! ASK MUM, DAD, OR WHOEVER LOOKS AFTER YOU TO HELP WITH SHARP KNIVES!

Oink! Let us show you how to make a Minecraft Pig sandwich. Mmmm... pig.

1 SQUARE EYES

MOBS MAY come and mobs may go, but the favourite Minecraft mob for many Minecraft fans will always be the pig! They're just so darn cute... and so tasty too! So for this Make It we're turning our faves into open sandwiches. You will need square bread, sliced ham, sliced cheese and chorizo, plus tomato sauce if you like it. Start by spreading sauce over your bread for some 'glue'! Now place a square of ham on your bread. Make some ham 'pixels' to place on top of it to give it that Minecraft look. Faces are 8x8 pixels, but these are too small, so we say cut your pixel squares to around 2cm in size. Then 2 strips of cheese for the base of the nose.

2 PORKY PIXELS

NOW OPEN up the chorizo and cut yourself four 'pixels' of the darker coloured piggy goodness. Place 2 either side of the nose, and two where your pig's eyes are going to be. Put a single ham 'pixel' in the centre of the nose and then add two cheese 'pixels' on the inside of the eyes to make up the square look of the eyeballs. Look at our handiwork here for the correct placement of all the pieces. You remember what a Minecraft pig looks like, right?

3 TOASTY GOODNESS!

YOU CAN either eat your Pig Open Sandwich cold (yeuck!) or pop it under the grill for about 5 minutes until the cheese melts and the chorizo goes all crispy around the edges. The sauce will warm through and the bread will toast around the edges too, giving you one delicious Minecraft Pig Open Sandwich that tastes like the most yummy pizza you ever had! Now scoff it.

PUZZLE ANSWERS

PAGE 14
SPOT THE DIFFERENCE
Check out the 6 differences in the photo...

PAGE 15
WHAT'S FOR TEA?
It was a GLISTERING MELON for tea!

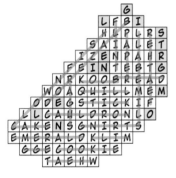

PAGE 16
WORD BLOCKS
1 = Villagers, 2 = Invisible, 3 = Dandelion,
4 = Endermite, 5 = Obtaining, 6 = Gunpower,
7 = Adventure, 8 = MossStone, 9 = Enchanted
The bonus word was = VIDEOGAME

PAGE 35
TRICKY CROSSING
Steve must first take the Chicken across
the river as the Wolf and the Bread are safe
together. He must leave the Chicken on the
other side and go back across. Now the Wolf
gets to ride in the boat, but Steve must bring
the Chicken back with him, as it will become
a snack for the Wolf if left together. He must
leave the Chicken on the other side, bringing
the Bread across this time, leaving it with
the Wolf. Now, finally, Steve can cross the
river, pick up the Chicken and end up with all
three of them on the other side of the river.
Easy, right?

HOW MANY BLOCKS?
There were 57 blocks left in the giant cube.

FIND THE WORD
It was SANDSTONE.

PAGE 52
SCOFF TIME
The CHICKEN is eating PUMPKIN PIE
The PIG is eating RAW CHICKEN
The RABBIT is eating CAKE
The WOLF is eating the APPLE
The POLAR BEAR is eating BREAD

TRACKBLOCKS
The words are:
GLOWSTONE
POISONOUS
CLOWNFISH

PAGE 53
MYSTERY MOB CRISS-CROSS
ACROSS: 5 = Elytra, 6 = Fishing Rod,
9 = String, 10 = Leather, 11 = Creative,
12 = Mojang, 13 = Story Mode.

DOWN: 1 = Crafting, 2 = The Nether, 3 = Baked
Potato, 4 = Mushroom, 5 = End Portal,
7 = Redstone, 8 = Ender Dragon, 10 = Llama.

The mystery mob was MOOSHROOM.

PAGE 57
MOB MAYHEM SEARCH
The mobs were:
Ghast, Magma Cube, Slime, Ender Dragon,
Ocelot, Parrot, Silverfish, Mooshroom,
Guardian, Squid, Enderman and Spider.

PAGE 71
HIDDEN ITEMS CRISS-CROSS
ACROSS: 1. Shears, 4. Iron Boots, 8. Puffer
Fish, 10. Emerald, 11. Shield, 12. Clock.

DOWN: 2. Eye Of Ender, 3. Cookie, 5. Slimeball,
6. Spawn Egg, 7. Nether Brick, 9. Saddle.
The mystery item is FLINT.

PAGE 75
WEAPON SUDOKU

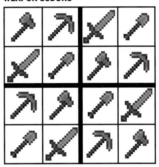

HOW MANY SPIDERS?
10

NAME THAT BLOCK
1 = Grass, 2 = Netherrack, 3 = Gold Ore,
4 = Magma, 5 = Redstone, 6 = Slime,
7 = TNT

PAGE 85
TRACKBLOCK
MINECRAFT, FLOWERPOT, BOOKSHELF

SPOT THE DIFFERENCE

HIDDEN BLOCKS
GRASS, MELON, SLIME, MAGMA

PAGE 90
ROUND 'N' ROUND CODE
The secret message is: REDSTONE POWERS
MINECRAFT.

HOW MANY PARROTS?
There were 12 parrots in the picture – two of
them hiding so you can only see part of them!

PAGE 91
FIND THAT BLOCK CRISS-CROSS
Across: 3 = Redstone Ore, 6 = Jack O'Lantern,
7 = Hay Bale, 8 = Sponge, 9 = Obsidian,
11 = Magma, 12 = TNT.

Down: 1 = Jukebox, 2 = Terracotta, 4 = Sticky
Piston, 5 = Bedrock, 10 = Snow.

The Mystery Mob is = ENDERMAN.

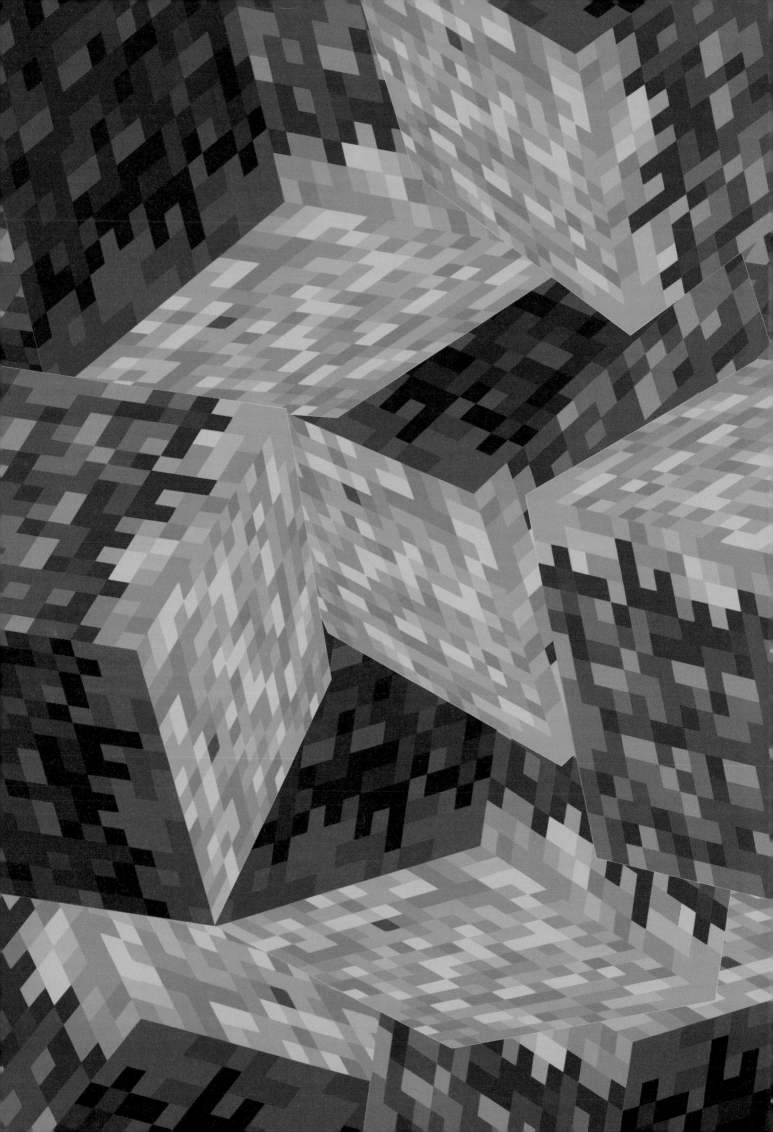